Fashion DIY

30 Ways to Craft Your Own Style

Ca

Sixth&Spring Books
233 Spring St.
New York, NY 10013

Vice President, Publisher
TRISHA MALCOLM

Editorial Director
ELAINE SILVERSTEIN

Art Director
CHI LING MOY

Book Editors
ERIN WALSH
AMANDA KEISER

Instructions Editors
PAT HARSTE
LINDA LEE

Book Division Manager
ERICA SMITH

Graphic Designers
SABRINA GUERRA
SHEENA T. PAUL

Production Manager
DAVID JOINNIDES

Photography
ROSE CALLAHAN
JACK DEUTSCH STUDIO

Fashion Stylists
MISTY GUNN
LAURA MAFFEO

Hair and Makeup
INGEBORG

Copy Editor
KRISTINA SIGLER

President, Sixth&Spring Books
ART JOINNIDES

Library of Congress Cataloging-in-Publication Data

Library of Congress Control Number: 2006931207
ISBN: 1-933027-18-5
ISBN-13: 978-1-933027-18-0

Manufactured in China

1 3 5 7 9 10 8 6 4 2

First Edition
2007

I have a deep, dark secret: I don't really know how to sew. Sure, I can run a folded fabric edge through my machine to hem it, but that's about all. Sewing a skirt or (even more intimidating) piecing together a shirt remains beyond my present abilities. As an embroidery artist, I wield a needle and thread 365 days a year, so it's a fair assumption that I could whip up some throw pillows if I had to. But when I was asked to write the foreword to the book you have in your hands, I thought...why me? I'm not a seamstress. Then, as I turned the pages, I realized that my skills naturally lend themselves to other realms of constructive sewing, and that the real focus of this book is what I love most: embellishment and unrestrained creativity.

In the last several years, a new generation has come of age that is keen on re-learning the handcrafting arts. As a result, these nearly bygone disciplines have begun to thrive and grow in exciting, unexpected ways. And we have discovered that even though sewing is no longer a necessity for most of us, working with our hands to create something personal and unique is as relevant as ever.

Thankfully for those of us with limited sewing skills, Carrie and Nicole's projects allow us to explore that creativity with little more than a knowledge of how to thread a needle. Explaining every step along the way, our crafty girls demonstrate how to transform garments with just a few key modifications. The techniques may be simple, but the results are stunning. Give a vintage dress new life by retrofitting it to your silhouette. See how something as simple as your choice of fabric can make an ordinary blouse spectacular. And never underestimate the effect of adding a strategically placed decorative button.

I've always wanted to get the basics of sewing down without having to endure the drudgery of a beginner's sewing book—and *Fashion DIY* is definitely the sugar that will make my sewing foot go down. While I'm busy playing with fun beads and trims, I have a feeling that I might accidentally learn a lot about sewing, too.

Jenny Hart

Embroidery artist and founder of Sublime Stitching,
www.sublimestitching.com

INTRODUCTION

I can remember the exact moment when I first awakened to the possibility of clothing embellishment and alteration. At age 13, already known for amassing vintage clothes, I received a 1970s dress from a friend's mother to add to my growing collection. The sleeves were all wrong and the neck was far too tight, but oh how I loved the fabric: wine-and-mustard-colored dotted swiss! My mother/ sewing-mentor listened to my lamentations, took a moment to examine the dress and simply said, "Well, then, I suppose we'll just make it sleeveless and create a new neckline."

I was electrified, amazed, excited! It was like a light bulb had permanently turned on in my head. No longer would it be necessary to "be satisfied" by the clothing I found and liked well enough, but that lacked a certain style cachet, was ill-fitting, or offered only one desirable element (like beautiful fabric). I could unlock the design potential in virtually any piece of clothing, new or vintage, no matter how hum-drum it might appear. The only limit was my imagination, and once the creativity started to flow, I found there was plenty to spare!

Nicole and I would like this book to unlock and inspire the same long-term devotion to embellishment in those who pick it up: Anyone can craft their own style with the techniques provided here. Although there is virtually no end to the

strategies and methods you can employ to alter your clothing, we have hammered out a list of the ten essential skill sets that you just can't live without. Each chapter will walk you through the basics of one skill, provide you with valuable information and resources you'll need to get started, and give you some practice with projects that are divided into three levels of difficulty.

The projects demonstrate the widely varying design options that the ten essential skills open up for you. Used as jumping-off points for your own creativity, the projects should be instructive but not rigid. Remember, this is about cultivating your unique style, so don't be afraid to dig in, learn the techniques and then strike out on your own.

Begin to explore by substituting elements of the existing projects: Create your own chiffon ruffle to adorn a slinky camisole instead of trimming a cardigan in ruched velvet, or incorporate reverse appliqué into the neckline of an elegant "little black dress" instead of a humble tee. Soon you'll have a handle on all ten skill sets and will find yourself ready to go forth and embellish using your new arsenal of creative strategies. You'll never look at your wardrobe the same way again!

Carrie Blaydes

FASHION DIY BASICS

One of the most liberating pieces of advice we've ever received was to "never look at a piece of clothing, a project-in-progress or a pile of scraps with finality." We've taken that advice to heart, and it has served us well throughout the years. It allows us the vision to hold up a 1940s tea dress in size XL and see the cute little cap-sleeved blouse we'll carve out of it. It helps us take a project that has veered off-course and simply follow the turning tide: A skirt ruined by miscalculations when creating a new hemline can be flipped upside down, stitched here and there, and sewn to a strap for an instant hobo bag. It also speaks to the packrat in us that relishes the excuse to hoard leftover bits of felted wool, fabrics and trim because "we can use that later!"

In many ways, the art of embellishment is all about problem solving. When you approach each project with an open mind and sense of humor, you will find that your designs become more creative and your process more rewarding.

We like to undertake a little "getting-to-know-you" session with each piece of clothing we set out to transform. Not only will it provide a loose road map for the project that saves time and frustration later on, but it will also help you to begin viewing almost any article of clothing as a candidate for greatness. That's our kind of thinking!

GETTING STARTED

1 Select a piece of clothing you want to embellish, such as:

a A thrift- or vintage-store find with great potential
b An old favorite that no longer fits
c Hand-me-downs from friends or relatives
d A retail item, sturdy and basic, that needs a style injection

2 Lay the garment flat, take a gander and ask yourself:

a Is this my size? Too large? Too small?
b Do I like the basic silhouette?
c What is the dominant color scheme? What colors would complement that dominant scheme well?
d Should I add embellishment or take away existing elements?
e Have I seen a similar garment with embellishment that I would like to recreate?
f Do I want to capture a particular look with this project (for example, 1950s retro, hippie-chic, etc.)?

3 Get out your tape measure and:

a Have a friend help you measure your bust, hips, waist, length from shoulder to shoulder and length of back from bottom of neck to true waist. Record these measurements and keep them handy for future reference.
b With the garment still laid flat, measure the same key areas. Remember to double the numbers! For example, if the waistband measures 15"/38cm across when laid flat, then the garment would fit a 30"/76cm waist.

4 Put pen to paper and:

a Make note of any sizing alterations you may need to perform on the garment. These should be taken care of before you proceed with the project.
b Do a quick sketch of the garment as it is now, then another sketch of your vision for the finished product. Make notes to one side about the steps you need to take to get from point A to point B—for example, if you want to shorten the sleeves, add pin-tucks to the waist area, add ribbon tie-backs, etc.

Now that you know where your project is headed, you should be ready to start. Gather your materials before you begin, put on some music you enjoy and get crafting!

TOOL BASICS

Stocking your sewing kit with the correct tools and supplies will help keep you frustration-free while crafting. Here's a list of useful tools you should always have handy to keep those projects running smoothly:

• Straight pins—make sure they are sharp; dull pins can snag delicate fabrics.

• Marking tools—tailor's chalk, water-soluble marking pens and fabric pencils all work well; just be sure to test them on your fabric before making any major marks.

• Fabric shears—keep a good pair of shears on hand that cut all the way to their tips. To keep blades sharp, never cut anything but fabric with your scissors.

• Hand-sewing needles—stock an assortment of needle lengths, thicknesses and eye sizes, and always dispose of dull needles.

• Pinking shears—a quick way to finish off a raw edge, pinking shears can save time or add decorative edges.

• Machine needles—always start a new project with a new machine needle.

• Extra bobbins—always replace cracked or warped bobbins, and use the type your machine requires.

• Thread—thread is available in myriad types and colors. Match your thread fiber content, care instructions and weight to that of your fabric as closely as possible.

FABRIC BASICS

• When searching for vintage textiles, keep your eyes peeled for obvious bonanzas like lengths of uncut yardage, but don't overlook other more readily available sources. Some of the best materials can be salvaged from home décor elements such as drapes or bedding, while vintage garments offer a dizzying array of beautiful patterns that can be reused in many different ways.

• It is always wise to wash fabrics before using them in craft projects, especially vintage textiles that may have been stored for lengthy periods of time. Use common sense when deciding whether to wash a vintage find or have it professionally cleaned. You can rely on the sturdiness of cotton, rayon and polyester to stand up to your machine's gentle cycle or a soak in Woolite, but you should leave all silks, wools, velvets and other fine fabrics to the able hands of your dry cleaner. Don't forget to press the fabric after washing! You should NEVER begin a project with wrinkled fabric!

• Never use bleach to brighten yellowed fabrics, since it can easily damage the fibers. As an alternative, try mixing a bath of Biz detergent that the fabric can soak in for up to a week, or using RIT dye in Bright White following the manufacturer's directions.

HAND-SEWING BASICS

Hand-sewing is one of the first skills you will need to embrace as you begin to embellish your clothing. It's useful for finishing certain machine-sewn projects, for making concealed stitches, for basting or for making stitches in hard-to-reach places where the machine simply cannot be utilized.

Commonly Used Stitches

1 Basting stitch
Typical uses: Creating temporary seams to hold pieces of fabric together, or to prepare any seam or hem that is about to receive a machine-stitched seam.

• Using a regular hand-sewing needle and thread in a contrasting color that can easily be seen against the background of the fabric, run your needle through the fabric along the seam line you have already marked using long-running stitches approximately ½"/1.3cm apart. Knot at both ends to secure.

Note Never skip this important step when preparing a project that will be machine-sewn. Failing to baste can result in mismatched ends and corners, uneven seams, puckering or problems with the garment's final fit.

2 Blanket and buttonholes stitches
See Chapter 1: Embroidery, "Getting Started."

3 Slipstitch

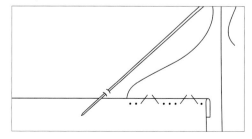

Typical use: Creating invisible hemlines.

• Fold the raw edge over ¼"/.6cm to the wrong side of the garment and press, then fold again to the desired hem width. Press again.

• Starting at a seam, bring your threaded needle through the folded hem, very close to the pressed edge (not the bottom edge), inserting the needle back through the hem approximately ⅜"/1cm to ¼"/.6cm away. Pluck the needle through the underneath fabric, making a tiny stitch that is barely visible (if at all) on the right side of the garment. Continue around the perimeter of the hemline.

4 Invisible stitch

Typical uses: When attaching certain kinds of trims, or any time you need to make hand-stitches that should not be seen.

• Bring needle through from wrong side of fabric. If attaching a trim, stitch once through the trim.

• Reinsert needle at almost the same point, carefully catching only a thread or two of the fabric itself.

• Move ⅜"/1cm to ¼"/.6cm on wrong side of fabric, bring needle up through right side once more, and repeat.

5 Catchstitch

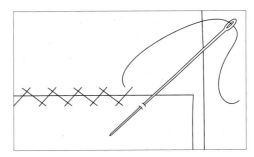

Typical uses: Hemming, holding two layers of fabric together while still allowing a degree of flexibility.

• Working from left to right (if you are right-handed), make a small stitch in the top layer of fabric close to the edge.

• Outside the edge of the upper layer, make the second stitch in the bottom layer of fabric diagonally across from the first stitch.

• Alternate stitching along the edge in a zigzag pattern, keeping threads loose.

MACHINE-SEWING BASICS

Although sewing machines are available in a wide range of prices, with an accompanying range of aptitudes and features, the good news is that a very basic machine (even a hand-me-down from decades ago) will allow you to perform all the necessary functions to create the projects in this book, as well as almost any embellishment projects you may undertake. This book assumes that you have a perfunctory knowledge of sewing machines (how to thread the needle and the bobbin, how to operate your stitch-dials and how to use the foot control to sew at different speeds). With that foundation and the basics of machine-sewing provided on the following pages, you should be well on your way to creating our projects and many of your own designs! And of course, when in doubt, check your machine's manual for priceless advice.

How To Make A Seam

1 If sewing two pieces of fabric together in a traditional seam, make sure you have the fabrics placed with right sides together and raw edges even.

2 Pin your fabric together along the seam line, or thread a needle and hand-sew a line of basting stitches along the seam line approximately ⅛"/.3cm away from the line itself. Make sure you have left enough seam allowance between the seam line and the raw edge. The standard seam allowance typically used in dress patterns is ⅝"/1.6cm. Most ready-to-wear garments are stitched using a ½"/1.3cm seam allowance.

3 Seam allowances are marked on the throat plate of virtually every sewing machine. If your machine does not have a mark on the throat plate for your preferred seam allowance, use a piece of masking tape to mark the spot.

4 Check all settings to ensure that you have your dials turned to the desired stitch pattern, width and length. Your settings will be determined by the type of fabric you use for each project. It always helps to experiment with different stitch settings on a scrap of the fabric you are using before you begin to sew on the garment itself. This can save you a lot of heartache!

5 Keeping raw edges even and lining up the fabric on the correct seam allowance mark on the throat plate, lower the presser foot and begin sewing. Never start stitching without lowering the presser foot. Stitch forward for ¼"/.6cm to ½"/1.3cm, then reverse-stitch (or backstitch) three to four stitches and begin sewing forward again along the seam line. This secures the stitches.

6 Keeping one hand on the fabric in front of the needle and one behind it, continue to sew along the seam line, being careful to remove the pins as you go so that you are not in danger of breaking your needle on one of them. Also be careful not to pull the fabric through. The machine will do the work as the fabric is stitched, any additional pulling from you can cause the fabric to pucker. Try to keep your foot very steady on the foot control so that the machine continues to sew at a regular, uniform speed.

7 When you reach the other end of your seam line, backstitch once again to secure the end.

8 Using a warm iron (with or without steam depending on your fabric), press your seam open so that the seam allowance lies flat. Pressing seams open as you sew them will always result in a more professional-looking final product.

9 To sew along any curves, make your notches or snips to adjust ease in the curve so that the pieces fit together properly, keeping raw edges even. It is also helpful to trim the curved part of the seam to ⅛"/.3cm before turning the garment right side out (see illustration on 15).

Commonly Used Machine Stitches

1 Basting stitch

Typical uses: Like hand-basting, machine-basting is typically used as a temporary stitch. It is particularly helpful for marking placement lines, temporarily holding two pieces together, or gathering ruffles and ruching.

• Set your machine to the straight stitch function and stitch using a longer length, typically five to six stitches per 1"/2.5cm.

2 Zigzag stitch

Typical uses: Applying appliqués, stitching buttonholes, finishing the raw edges of seams and attaching elastic.

• Wider zigzags tend to pull in the fabric with each stitch. Using a multi-step zigzag stitch for wider stitching, which forms multiple stitches between zigzags, will help alleviate any unwanted puckering.

• Always attach the proper foot before beginning your stitches. Using the wrong foot may result in the needle hitting the foot and breaking.

3 Satin stitch

Typical use: Applying appliqués and decorative details.

• Adhere stabilizer to the back of the fabric to eliminate puckering.

• Set your machine to the zigzag stitch function and attach the proper foot. Adjust machine settings to approximately sixty stitches per 1"/2.5cm. The example shown has slightly fewer stitches per inch so that the stitches are not touching.

• Adjust stitch width to your liking.

4 Blind hem stitch

Typical use: Hemming woven fabrics to create a hidden row of stitches from the outside of the garment.

• Attach the blind hem foot to the machine if available. The foot isn't necessary but is very helpful when stitching a blind hem.

• Consult your machine's instruction manual for folding the fabric properly and feeding it into the machine.

5 Overlock stitch

Typical use: Finishing raw edges.

• Set machine to overlock stitch and attach the appropriate foot.

• Feed the fabric into the machine with the straight stitches running very close to, or along, the raw edge of the fabric.

6 Feather stitch

Typical uses: Topstitching lace or attaching two fabrics that are butted up against each other.

• Set machine to the feather stitch and attach the appropriate foot (some machines may refer to this stitch at the faggoting stitch).

• Pin two fabrics together with raw edges butted against each other, but not overlapping.

• Feed the fabric into the machine with the raw edges centered under the needle so that the sides of the feather stitch catch both pieces of fabric.

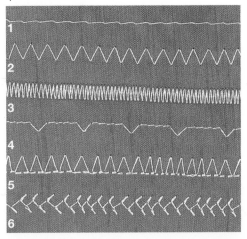

7 Blanket stitch

Typical use: Finishing raw edges.

• Set machine to the blanket stitch and attach the appropriate foot.

• Feed the fabric into the machine with the straight stitches of the blanket stitch running along the raw edge.

8 Honeycomb stitch

Typical uses: Creating gathers for smocking and attaching elastic bands.

• Use this stitch for a decorative way to topstitch cording yarn or ribbon.

9 Scalloped edge stitch

Typical use: Decorative stitching.

• Create a dainty hem finish by stitching the scalloped edge near the bottom hem of your garment. Trim away excess fabric along the bottom edge of the stitching.

Making a sturdy seam

There are two different ways you can reinforce the seam you have just made in order to ensure that your work will stand up to normal wear and washing for years to come.

Method 1 Working on the ⅝"/1.6cm seam allowance you left when creating your initial seam, sew a zigzag stitch adjacent to the seam and then trim very close to the zigzag stitches.

Method 2 Working on the ⅝"/1.6cm seam allowance, make a straight seam approximately ¼"/.6cm from the fabric edge, then use pinking shears to trim very close to those stitches.

General tips and techniques

• When sewing stretchy fabrics such as jersey knits (what most T-shirts are made of), use a zigzag stitch or one of your machine's stretch settings. This will allow for some give in your stitches, making them less likely to break during the course of normal wear.

• Hold both your bobbin and needle threads in your hand for your first three to four stitches of any seam. This will prevent your bobbin thread from balling up into a mess on the underside of your seam.

• A technique called pivoting should be used when you reach a corner in your sewing. Simply sew right up to the corner, lower your needle into the fabric to hold it in place, raise your presser foot, pivot the fabric according to your seam line, then lower the presser foot again and continue sewing in the new direction.

tip Experiment with stitching numerous widths and lengths of the various stitches on your machine. Label the stitches and keep handy for a quick and useful reference during future projects.

• When sewing a curved seam, use clipping to adjust ease [see illustration below], as follows:

For an inside curve (A), trim the seam allowance and then make snips in the seam allowance (right up to the edge of the seam placement) every ¼"/.6cm to ½"/1.3cm, depending on the degree of curve.

For an outside curve (B), trim the seam allowance to ⅛"/.3mm.

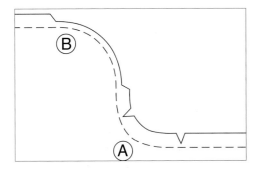

Choosing a needle

Machine needles are sold in sizes that are indicated in fractions—the higher the number, the larger the needle. The first number in the fraction indicates the needle's diameter in millimeters, and the second number is the standard U.S. needle size.

General needle guide

Silk fabrics	60/8
Lightweight fabrics	70/10
Medium-weight fabrics	80/12
Medium- to heavyweight fabrics	90/14
Heavyweight fabrics	100/16
Upholstery fabrics	110/18

Choosing a thread

Thread is the only thing holding your precious creations together, so look for quality when purchasing threads. Lower-quality threads will appear fuzzy and will break in your machine or after minimal wear and tear. Not all threads are created equally—you definitely get what you pay for.

For the best color match, unwind a few inches of the thread, lay it over your fabric and select a hue one shade darker. Lighter shades of thread will leave a more noticeable seam on the finished product.

1 EMBROIDERY

GETTING STARTED

Designing supplies

- Tracing paper, carbon and/or transfer paper
- Pencil and/or sharp point (to do transfer)
- Paper scissors
- Ruler
- Masking tape
- Straight pins
- Photocopy machine (for resizing images)

Sewing supplies

- Embroidery hoop
- Stabilizer
- Embroidery needles in appropriate sizes (ribbon embroidery needles for ribbonwork)
- Floss/thread/ribbon (depending upon project)
- Fabric scissors, embroidery snips
- Thimble
- Tape measure
- Straight pins
- Water-soluble marking pen

Thread Options

- Stranded cotton (commonly known as embroidery floss)—contains six strands per thread
- Stranded silk—contains up to twelve strands
- Cotton perle (or pearl cotton)—a twisted cotton thread available in various thicknesses
- Silk ribbons—usually no more than ⅜"/1cm in thickness, but there are some exceptions to this rule

- Wool yarns—tapestry yarn (the thickest), contains four strands, and crewel wool yarn (the thinnest), contains two strands

Fabrics

Almost any material will work as your ground fabric, but always use a stabilizer (preferably wash- or tear-away) to ensure perfect stitches when working with knits or stretchy fabrics like T-shirts. Never stretch the fabric larger than its normal size, or your design will appear scrunched or distorted when removed from the hoop. And remember: Don't skip the stabilizer!

Transferring designs

1 Reduce or enlarge your image to the desired size using a photocopier. Trace the design onto tracing paper.

2 Place fabric on a hard, flat surface.

3 Tape tracing paper to a piece of transfer or carbon paper, with the transfer/carbon side down.

4 Place the two pieces of paper on your fabric with the transfer/carbon side down and touching the fabric. Use two pins to secure the papers in place so they don't shift as you transfer the image. Remember to use only two pins to minimize the risk of them causing unwanted transfer marks.

5 Using a very sharp pencil or pointy object, carefully trace over your design. Press hard enough to transfer the image fully, but not so hard that you tear the tracing paper.

6 Remove one pin and lift up a corner of the paper (leaving the other pin in place to prevent the papers from shifting) to make sure that the entire design has transferred properly before you remove the papers. This step is necessary because it is very difficult to place the paper in precisely the same position once it has been moved. If the transfer was not complete, lay papers back into position and retrace the image using your sharp point.

How to start and finish

1 Select the needle for the type of embroidery and thread that you are using, and thread the needle with the appropriate number of strands.

2 The type of stitches used determines whether to knot the threads to begin and end. When stitching straight lines such as a stem stitch, knot the threads. When sewing fill-type stitches, such as satin stitching, it is not necessary to knot the threads.

3 To begin, bring the thread to the right side and take one or two very small tack stitches to secure the stitching. Hold the thread tail with one hand on the back side of the project and work the thread tail into the stitches as you sew.

4 To end, take the needle to the back side of the project, tie a knot if necessary and run the needle under a few stitches to secure the stitching and hide the thread tail. Clip close to the stitching.

Embroidering with ribbon

• Working with shorter lengths of ribbon (less than 20"/51cm at a time) will help to prevent wrinkling and twisting that can ruin the final effect of the embroidery. While ribbon widths can vary, a 4–7mm size will perform best in the creation of petals and leaves.

• Although polyester and other synthetic versions are available, 100 percent silk is the preferred material for embroidery ribbon. Silks lend themselves well to the desired organic look and texture of the finished product, often a floral motif, and are available in almost any color.

• For a modern take on ribbon embroidery, try cutting strips of fabric to embroider with. If the strips can pass through the fabric with a needle without causing damage, you can embroider with them!

Commonly used embroidery stitches

1 Chain stitch

Typical uses: Outlines, lettering, borders and frames. Usually uses two strands of embroidery floss, sometimes three.

2 French knot

Typical uses: Flower centers, dotted details, borders. Usually uses two strands of embroidery floss.

3 Running stitch

Typical uses: Accent colors, borders and frames. Uses up to three strands of embroidery floss, depending on desired thickness of stitches.

4 Backstitch

Typical uses: Accent colors, outlines and detailing, borders and frames. Uses up to three strands of embroidery floss, depending on desired thickness of line.

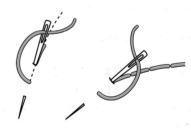

5 Satin stitch

Typical uses: Filling in areas with color, creating shapes like leaves, rather than lines. Uses up to three strands of embroidery floss, depending on the desired look of the design and the thread being used, since shinier threads such as stranded silk are commonly employed for this stitch.

6 Blanket stitch

Typical uses: Similar to buttonhole stitch, but more commonly used for finishing edges and going around the edges of an appliqué. Uses up to three strands of embroidery floss.

7 Outline stitch (also known as stem stitch)

Typical uses: Outlines, stems of flowers, borders and lettering. Uses up to three strands of embroidery floss.

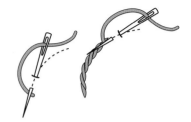

8 Fly stitch

Typical uses: Outlines, borders and frames. Usually uses two strands of embroidery floss and sometimes three.

9 Lazy daisy stitch

Typical uses: Stitching flowers and large petals. Uses up to three strands of embroidery floss.

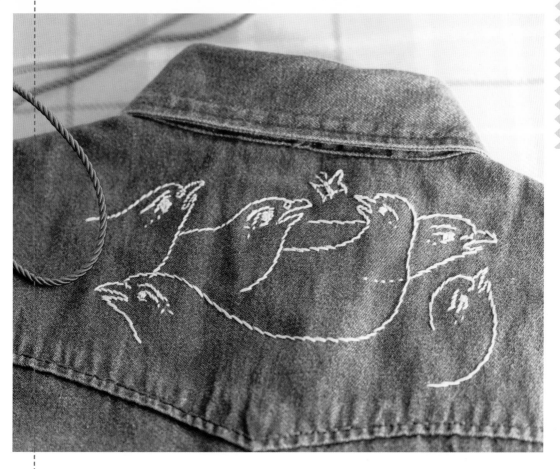

Calamity Jane Top

EASY

Whether you live in Denver, Colorado, or in Queens, New York, this Western-inspired shirt is a perfect way to add relaxed country style to your wardrobe. Choose vibrant colors for a rodeo-ready statement, or select more muted tones for a subtle nod to the ranch.

Supplies

- Denim Western-style shirt
- Computer
- Printer and paper
- Tracing paper
- Transfer paper
- Pen
- Embroidery floss in purple
- Embroidery floss in cream
- Embroidery needle
- Embroidery hoop
- Embroidery scissors

Calamity Jane Top

1 Using a computer, print out a letter in desired font and size. Transfer letter to the left yoke of the shirt.

2 Mount shirt yoke into the embroidery hoop. Thread embroidery needle with two strands of cream floss, knotting at one end. Embroider letter using backstitch. Tie off floss and trim excess. Remove shirt from embroidery hoop.

3 Using a computer, print out a bird motif in desired size. Transfer motif to the center of the back yoke.

4 Mount shirt yoke into the embroidery hoop. Thread embroidery needle with two strands of cream floss, knotting at one end. Embroider bird motif using the stem stitch. Tie off floss and trim excess. Remove blouse from embroidery hoop.

5 Thread needle with three strands of purple embroidery floss and knot one end. Using a running stitch, stitch along both edges of the front button placket, around the edges of the cuffs and along the bottom of the back and front yokes. Tie off floss and trim excess.

tip The Internet is a fantastic resource where you can find images and clip art available to download. We purchased the bird motif image online at www.missmary.com.

Lady Victoria Cuff

MODERATE

A little bit lady and a little bit rock-n-roll, this clever embroidered cuff can accessorize anything from a cocktail dress to jeans. If the cameo isn't your style, use a star, a paisley, or even a guitar. Any design you can trace is a candidate for embroidery!

Supplies

- 2"/5cm-wide brass cuff
- 12"/30.5cm square of organza in white
- Embroidery floss in cream
- Embroidery floss in black
- Metallic embroidery floss in bronze
- Fabri-Tac adhesive
- Dazzle-It Wand
- Pearl Dazzle-It jewels
- Embroidery needle
- Embroidery hoop
- Embroidery scissors
- Water-soluble marking pen

1 Trace cameo template onto organza with water-soluble marking pen.

2 Mount organza into embroidery hoop. Thread embroidery needle with one strand of black embroidery floss and knot one end. Embroider the outline of the cameo head using a backstitch. Tie off thread and trim excess.

3 Thread embroidery needle with two strands of black floss and knot one end. Fill in the head motif with satin stitches. Tie off thread and trim excess.

4 Thread embroidery needle with one strand of bronze floss and knot one end. Embroider the outline of the border using backstitch. Tie off thread and trim excess.

5 Thread embroidery needle with two strands of bronze floss and fill border with satin stitches, with the stitches piercing just outside the outline stitch. Tie off thread and trim excess.

6 Thread embroidery needle with two strands of cream floss. Fill background of motif with satin stitches.

7 Remove organza from embroidery hoop and cut out cameo motif using embroidery scissors.

8 Using Fabri-Tac, adhere cameo to the cuff in the desired location.

9 Using Dazzle-It Wand, adhere pearls around the cameo following the manufacturer's directions.

tip This technique can be used to make embroidered embellishments to adhere to otherwise hard-to-stitch surfaces such as belt buckles, leather purses and shoes.

Secret Garden Skirt

INVOLVED

Until recently, ribbon embroidery was a forgotten relic art. One look at this lovely skirt, however, and you can see why stylish needle-wielders are rediscovering the art of embroidering with silk ribbon. What says summer better than this sweet floral design?

Supplies

- Box-pleated skirt
- Bucilla 4mm silk embroidery ribbon, three packages in pale hunter and one package each in federal blue, deep red and light pink
- Bucilla 7mm silk embroidery ribbon, one package in

- pale honey
- White thread
- Tear-away stabilizer
- Ribbon embroidery needle
- Hand-sewing needle
- Embroidery hoop

- Embroidery scissors
- Water-soluble marking pen (optional)
- Transfer paper and sharp pencil (optional)
- Photocopier

Make large red and pink flowers

1 For each flower (number will depend on the number of box pleats on the front of your skirt; the supply list assumes four flowers), prepare the following: five 2"/5cm pieces of red ribbon, five 2"/5cm pieces of pink ribbon, one 5"/12.5cm piece of honey ribbon, one ¾"/1.9cm square of tear-away stabilizer, hand-sewing needle threaded with white thread.

2 Tie a fairly loose knot in the center of each 2"/5cm piece of ribbon.

3 Fold one 2"/5cm piece of red ribbon so that the two ends overlap to make a petal shape with the knot at the petal's tip.

4 Using hand-sewing needle and white thread, stitch petal to a small square (slightly larger than the center of the flower) of stabilizer at the point where the two ends overlap in the center. The result should be a petal approximately ¾"/1.9cm long from stitch line to tip [see illustration, right]. Using embroidery scissors, cut away excess ribbon beyond stitch line.

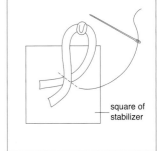

square of stabilizer

5 Repeat steps 2 and 3 for remaining red ribbons to make a five-petal flower shape on the square of stabilizer.

6 Follow steps 2 and 3 for five pink ribbon petals as well, centering each pink ribbon between the red petals and stitching approximately ¼"/.6cm shorter than the red petals.

7 Tightly twist one end of pale honey ribbon between thumb and forefinger, then stitch twisted tip to the center of the circular petal arrangement [see illustration right].

8 Twist remaining ribbon more loosely, spiraling it to form a small yellow rosette in the center of the flower.

9 Hold rosette tightly under thumb to keep in place while securing from underneath with very tiny stitches. When finished, securely knot thread.

10 Trim excess honey ribbon with embroidery scissors.

11 Tear away excess stabilizer, using caution not to disturb stitches.

12 Make as many large flowers as desired (supply list assumes four), set aside.

Embroider the skirt

1 Use water-soluble marking pen or tracing paper, transfer paper and a sharp pencil to lay out embroidery motif on fabric. The motif should be positioned so that the vine begins at the top of the box pleat. Freehand embroidery without marked guidelines of the motif can also be employed (as in the example shown) if a precisely uniform effect is not preferred.

2 Unfold box pleat to open and secure with pins if necessary before placing in embroidery hoop. With hoop firmly in place, thread hunter ribbon onto ribbon embroidery needle, knotting one end, and use a backstitch to create the vine.

3 Add as many leaves as desired, using ¼"/.6cm to ½"/1.3cm single stitches and being careful to keep ribbon untwisted so that the leaves appear full. When finished, knot hunter ribbon, but do not remove embroidery hoop.

4 Thread ribbon embroidery needle with an 8"/20.5cm piece of blue ribbon and knot at one end.

5 Embroider a four-petal lazy daisy stitch flower to one side of the vine. To create each petal, bring the needle up through fabric, then reinsert right next to the point of emergence, being careful not to pull tight but instead to leave a ½"/1.3cm loop on the right side of the fabric. Next, bring needle back up through fabric approximately ½"/1.3cm above the base of the loop. Wrap stitch around the loop and bring needle to the wrong side of the fabric. Pull tight to secure petal. Repeat to create three additional petals.

6 Remove embroidery hoop and repeat steps 1–6 on additional box pleats.

7 Using hand-sewing needle and white thread, stitch one large flower at the bottom of each vine. Stitch the center piece of stabilizer to the skirt and tack the knot of each petal.

8 Press skirt to remove embroidery hoop marks.

A Pale Hunter (4mm)
B Federal Blue (4mm)
C Deep Red (4mm)
D Lt. Pink (4mm)
E Pale Honey (7mm)

tip Depending on the number of box pleats your skirt has, it may be preferable to embroider only the front pleats. Another attractive design option is to embroider the motif on every other pleat.

GETTING STARTED

Basic supplies

- Appliqué or piece of fabric to be appliquéd
- Paper-backed fusible webbing
- Thread
- Hand-sewing needle
  (if appliqué is to be hand-sewn)
- Embroidery hoop (if appliqué is to be hand-sewn)
- Sewing machine
- Embroidery or other small scissors

Preparing an appliqué from fabric

1 Lay appliqué fabric face down on a hard, flat surface or directly on your ironing board.

2 Following the manufacturer's instructions, lay a sheet of fusible webbing on the wrong side of the fabric (paper side up) and press a warm iron over the surface to fuse the webbing to the fabric.

3 Cut your appliqué from the fabric in the desired shape, using a design template if desired.

4 Remove paper backing, place appliqué carefully on garment in desired final location, then press with a warm iron to fuse the fabrics together. When adhering appliqués with fusible stabilizer, press the iron and hold the iron in place. Do not slide the iron around as if you were ironing a garment. Lift iron to reposition and press again where necessary.

Hand appliqué

1 Stretch fabric (with appliqué already fused in place) into embroidery hoop, centering the appliqué in the hoop to make stitching around all edges possible.

2 Stitch around all edges of fabric using blanket or buttonhole stitch.

Machine satin stitch appliqué

1 Secure tear- or wash-away stabilizer to the back of your background fabric by using a fusible variety or temporary spray adhesive. (Satin stitch will pucker without the use of a stabilizer.)

2 Set machine to either a very close zigzag stitch or a buttonhole stitch setting to create a satin stitch. Try various stitch widths on a test swatch to achieve the desired width. The larger your appliqué, the wider your satin stitch should be.

3 Slowly work a line of satin stitches around the edges of the appliqué, turning the fabric very carefully to avoid puckering.

4 If your appliqué has corners, you must pivot around them as follows: When you reach a corner, simply remove your foot from the foot control and manually turn the wheel to lower the needle into the fabric. Lift the presser foot and turn the fabric to the desired direction. Then lower the presser foot and continue sewing.

Asia Minor Skirt

EASY

Express your personal style by creating unique, one-of-a-kind appliqués using any fabric or shape that captures your imagination. Here a floral motif from some leftover rayon yardage was chosen, but you can just as easily make candy-striped hearts, oversized flowers in bold solids or even a soaring cloud-print bird.

Supplies

- Skirt
- Fabric with desired motif(s)
- ½yd/.5m of Wonder Under (more may be needed if your motif is larger)

- Contrasting thread
- Small craft scissors

- Iron
- Sewing machine

1 Cut a piece of Wonder Under slightly larger than the size of the fabric motif. Position the Wonder Under on the wrong side of the fabric motif. Following the manufacturer's instructions, press with the iron to adhere the Wonder Under to the fabric. Do not remove the paper backing.

2 Cut appliqué motif from the fabric, cutting through the Wonder Under and the fabric.

3 Remove paper backing from Wonder Under, then place appliqué in desired location on the skirt. Press with the iron to adhere to the skirt.

4 Stitch around the edges of the appliqué with long and narrow zigzag stitches.

5 Repeat for additional appliqués.

tip Appliqués can be made from any fabric, from a wardrobe favorite featuring a beloved print that no longer fits or from a garment with an unsightly stain that can't be hidden under its own appliqué.

Mozambique Tee

MODERATE

Inspired by traditional African fabrics, this reverse appliquéd T-shirt has a slightly flirty flair thanks to sheer chiffon in vibrant colors. Almost any fabric can be chosen for the revealed design, allowing for endless variety in the use of this technique.

Supplies

- Brown T-shirt
- 12"/30.5cm squares of chiffon in red and dark teal
- Tear-away stabilizer
- Temporary spray adhesive
- Water-soluble marking pen
- Embroidery floss in white
- Embroidery needle
- Embroidery scissors
- Embroidery hoop
- Tape measure
- Cardboard for templates

1 Trace triangle shapes provided and create cardboard templates.

2 Using tape measure and marking pen, place the large template at the center front neckline and mark position, then mark appropriate location of three small triangles around the neckline on both sides.

3 Layer a square of red chiffon underneath the area marked for the large triangle on the inside of the T-shirt and pin in place. Using spray adhesive, adhere a square of stabilizer underneath the chiffon. Make sure that the chiffon is layered between the T-shirt and the stabilizer.

4 Mount the T-shirt into the embroidery hoop with the triangle in the hoop. Using neat, even backstitches, hand-sew around the marked perimeter of the triangle.

5 Tear away stabilizer from outer edge of stitching, then carefully make a small tear in the center of the stitched triangle and use embroidery scissors to cut away stabilizer from behind chiffon triangle, cutting as closely as possible inside the stitch lines without damaging the chiffon. Trim excess chiffon outside the margins of the stitch lines.

6 Repeat steps 2 and 3, using teal chiffon for each of the six smaller triangles.

7 Remove T-shirt from embroidery hoop. Use thumb and forefinger to carefully separate the T-shirt material from the chiffon behind it, then use embroidery scissors to make a small snip in the center of each T-shirt triangle only.

8 Using embroidery scissors, slowly cut away jersey fabric from inside the stitch lines of each triangle, leaving a margin of jersey approximately ⅛"/.3cm deep inside the stitch perimeter.

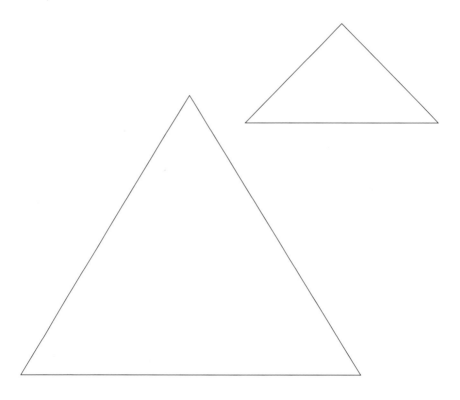

tip Don't like revealing chiffon? Try cotton calicos for a pretty patchwork look, or even gold lamé for a striking nightlife showstopper.

Yacht Club Dress

INVOLVED

Take the guesswork out of getting ready with this pre-accessorized dress! Appliquéd fabric "buttons" inject the nondescript denim with a classic nautical feel, while the attached sash completes the look. Bon voyage!

Supplies

- Dress with a plain front and back zipper
- 1 yd/1m solid dark red fabric
- Tear-away stabilizer
- Matching dark red thread
- White thread

- Pattern or tissue paper
- Ruler
- Fabric scissors
- Pen
- Compass or 1¼"/3cm diameter circle template

- Measuring tape
- Water-soluble marking pen or tailor's chalk
- Glue stick
- Iron
- Sewing machine

37

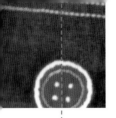

Yacht Club Dress

1 Lay dress down on a flat working surface. Lay pattern paper down over the waistline of the dress. Draw sash to desired width onto the pattern paper using the ruler as a guide. Trace the sides of the dress for the sides of the belt.

2 Turn dress over and repeat step 1 for the back.

3 Using the ruler, add a ¼"/.6cm seam allowance around all edges of the front belt piece.

4 Cut out back piece and cut in half crosswise (where the zipper is). Tape one back piece to another pattern paper and trace ¼"/.6cm outside of all the edges, creating a ¼"/.6cm seam allowance.

5 Using the new back pattern piece, cut two back belt pieces from the red fabric. Cut one front belt piece from the red fabric.

6 Pin the short ends of the back sash pieces to the front piece with right sides together and raw edges even. Stitch with a ¼"/.6cm seam allowance to create the sash.

7 Turn all edges of the sash under ¼"/.6cm and press in place. Pin the sash to the dress and slipstitch in place using small stitches with dark red thread.

8 Using contrasting white thread, machine-stitch a straight stitch ¼"/.6cm above the bottom edge of the sash. Stitch another line ¼"/.6cm above this stitch line. Repeat until the entire width of the sash is stitched in place with parallel lines.

9 Using measuring tape, find the center front of the dress. Mark a line with the water-soluble marking pen down the center of the dress from the neckline to the top of the sash.

10 Mark six button appliqué placements with water-soluble marking pen or tailor's chalk, making sure they are evenly spaced along the center front.

11 Cut six circles for button appliqués 1¼"/3cm in diameter from dark red fabric. Place button appliqués on their marked placements and pin (a dab of glue will help keep the circles in place while sewing).

12 Place a layer of tear-away stabilizer behind the button appliqués on the "wrong" side of the dress and pin in place.

13 Satin stitch around the edges of all the buttons.

14 Using water-soluble marking pen or tailor's chalk, draw a smaller circle and four "holes" inside the satin-stitched frame of each button appliqué.

15 Using a straight stitch on the machine, stitch each smaller circle on all button appliqués.

16 At marked "holes," hand-stitch a few stitches in white thread, or create each "hole" with a French knot.

17 Tear away stabilizer from the backside of the dress front and remove any placement marks.

tip For added detail on the sash, try adding another appliqué in the shape of a belt buckle.

3 TRIMMING

GETTING STARTED

Basic supplies

- Trim
- Sewing machine
- Yardstick or ruler
- Water-soluble marking pen, tailor's chalk, or white water-soluble marking pencil
- Tape measure
- Straight pins
- Water-soluble fabric tape (optional)

Basic types of trim

- Ribbon—grosgrain, silk, taffeta, organza, velvet, satin, novelty, etc.

- Lace—can be acquired new or vintage, in varying widths and several different base materials such as cotton, acetate, silk or polyester. May be machine-woven, laser-cut, machine- or hand-crocheted, or even hand-tatted or knotted.

- Rickrack

- Piping

- Gimp—a heavyweight trim made from artfully looped cording, usually seen in home décor projects.

- Specialty trims—beaded or sequined, ribbon with tiny silk flowers attached, flocked materials, fringe, etc.

- Elastics—sometimes utilized as trims.

Basic trimming techniques

1 Measure the proper length of trim you will need to complete each portion of the project, adding a 2"/5cm allowance for each piece. Cut the trim into pieces according to these measurements and set aside.

2 Using a yardstick, ruler or other straightedge, use your water-soluble marking pen, marking pencil or tailor's chalk to precisely mark the line on your fabric where you would like to place the trim. If desired, adhere fabric tape along marked line.

3 Pin trim to markings or adhere to fabric tape, making sure to turn under the two ends of the trim approximately ½"/1.3cm so that you will have finished ends.

4 Machine-stitch trim to garment using desired machine setting. **Note** When using flat trims such as grosgrain ribbon, it may be desirable to allow your machine stitches to become a part of the embellishment. To create this effect, select thread in a contrasting color that complements the trim, set your machine to the zigzag or another novelty stitch, and create the seam directly down the center of the ribbon.

5 Repeat steps 2–4 for all areas of the garment you would like to trim.

6 If desired, wash garment following manufacturer's instructions in order to dissolve the fabric tape.

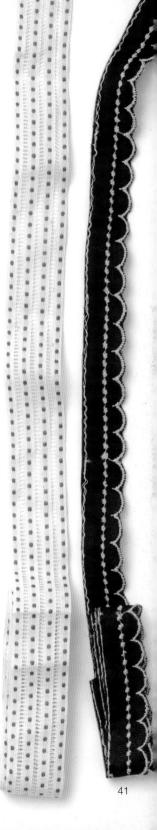

Domino Dress

EASY

Rickrack, a childhood favorite, suddenly appears all grown up when peeking from behind the edges of this elegant belted dress. A classic pairing of crisp black cotton with graphic white detail, this project elevates humble rickrack to design greatness while stylishly transforming an otherwise forgettable off-the-rack dress.

Supplies

- Black dress with collar and sash
- Wrights ½"/1.3cm-wide "medium rickrack" in white
- Black thread
- Dritz Fray Check
- Straight pins
- Measuring tape
- Sewing machine

1 Measure along all edges of the dress where you would like to add rickrack to determine the yardage of rickrack needed. **Note** Wrights ½"/1.3cm-wide medium rickrack comes in 2½yd/2.3m packages. Be sure to purchase enough packages to equal yardage needed, plus approximately 24"/61cm more. When cutting pieces of rickrack to pin to the dress, be sure to allow yourself a few extra inches/centimeters per piece to allow for any miscalculations.

2 Measure around the collar edge; make note of measurement. Cut a piece of rickrack the same measurement, plus a few extra inches/centimeters.

3 Pin rickrack around the collar with half of the rickrack on the wrong side of the collar. Machine-stitch in place, close to the edge of the collar [see illustration, right]. Trim off excess and apply Fray Check to raw edges.

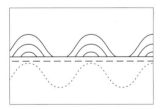

4 Measure along one side of the neckline and cut a piece of rickrack the same measurement, plus a few extra inches/centimeters. Pin rickrack to the inside of the neckline with half of the trim extending out over the edge. Machine-stitch in place, close to the edge of the neckline. Trim excess rickrack and apply Fray Check to raw edges.

5 Repeat step 4 for the other side of the neckline.

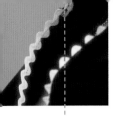

Domino Dress

6 Measure around the edges of one sash and cut a length of rickrack the same measurement, plus several inches/centimeters. Pin rickrack to the wrong side of the sash's edges with half of the trim extending out over the edge. Machine-stitch in place, close to the edge of the fabric. Trim excess rickrack and apply Fray Check to raw edges.

7 Repeat step 6 for the other sash.

tip If the dress has tabs around the sleeve cuffs, as here, be sure to pin the rickrack trim to the wrong side of the tab, so when the tab is folded up, only the rickrack peeking from under the edges will be seen.

Mind Your Manners Cardigan

MODERATE

Simple and elegant, the ruched velvet cuffs on this cardigan could just as easily update a wool coat for winter. Brilliant in its simplicity, the technique can also be used to create ruched or ruffled trims out of almost any ribbon or fabric you choose.

Supplies

- Cardigan sweater
- 1yd/1m of velvet ribbon between 1½"/4cm and 3"/7.5cm wide
- Polyester thread
- Hand-sewing needle
- Straight pins
- Fabric scissors
- Tape measure
- Sewing machine

1 Using tape measure, determine circumference of sleeve openings; make note of measurement.

2 Depending on density of velvet ribbon's pile and the softness of its backing, multiply sleeve opening circumference by two (for denser/thicker/stiffer ribbon) or three (for thinner/softer ribbon). Using this measurement, cut two lengths of ribbon (one for each sleeve).

3 Using sewing machine, baste a straight seam as close to the ribbon's edge as possible, backstitching at one end (it is preferable to place these seams on the narrow selvage running down either side, as shown in this example). Repeat on both edges of each ribbon. **Note** It is important not to secure these seams using the typical method of machine backstitching on both ends. Instead, leave seams unsecured at one end with several inches/centimeters of extra seam and bobbin thread hanging loose.

4 Holding tightly onto the loose top thread (not the bobbin thread), pull the ribbon along the thread so that it begins to draw up along the edge. Be careful not to pull too quickly or sharply, as it will create too much tension and cause the threads to break. Continue until the edge of the ribbon has been drawn up to the circumference of the sleeve plus 1"/2.5cm. At this point the ribbon will look like a ruffle. If measurements do not match, continue pulling to increase ruching and shorten length, or loosen ruching slightly to increase length. Knot thread to secure ruching. Repeat process to gather the other side of the ribbon. The finished product should be fully ruched and measure approximately one-half to one-third of its original length.

5 Repeat step 4 to ruche second length of ribbon.

6 Beginning at a seam, turn under one end of ruched trim ½"/1.3cm and secure with a pin so that the bottom edge of the trim and the bottom edge of the cardigan's sleeve opening line up exactly.

tip To make ruffled trims, follow steps 1–4, making a seam only on one edge of the ribbon rather than on both edges. Lace works particularly well for ruffles, while sequined or beaded trims should be avoided.

7 Hand-sew ruched trim along edge of sleeve opening using small, hidden stitches. Repeat along upper edge of trim.

8 Turn under final end of trim ½"/1.3cm when it is reached, then slipstitch the two ends together, working from the inside with small, hidden stitches.

9 Repeat steps 6–8 to create other cuff.

Art School Skirt

INVOLVED

This smart wrap skirt offers graphic sophistication without taking itself too seriously. To enjoy freedom of choice, make your own bias tape using a cotton fabric like the pinstripe shown here. Or, go the easier route by using packaged bias tape or other trims, and get a look you're sure to love.

Supplies

- Wrap skirt
- 1yd/1m of black-and-white-striped fabric
- White thread
- Water-soluble marking pen or tailor's chalk
- Ruler
- Scissors
- Rotary mat and rotary cutter (optional)
- Iron
- Sewing machine

1 Cut six 2"/5cm-wide strips of striped fabric on the bias. The bias is at a 45-degree angle to the selvage of the fabric, so you will be cutting strips at a diagonal on the fabric [see Figure 1]. **Note** You can map out your strips with a water-soluble marking pen and cut them out with scissors, or you can use a ruler, rotary cutter and mat for quicker cutting.

2 Cut five 1½"/4cm-wide strips of fabric on the bias.

3 With right sides together and short ends even, stitch two 2"/5cm-wide bias strips together at an angle. Trim seam allowance to ¼"/.6cm and press [see Figure 2].

4 Make one long strip of bias tape with the remaining four strips of 2"/5cm-wide bias strips, stitching them together in the same method as step 3.

5 Make one continuous strip out of four 1½"/4cm-wide bias strips, stitching them together with the same method as step 3.

6 To turn bias strips into double-fold bias tape, fold strip in half lengthwise and press. Next, turn long raw edges under to the center fold and press, encasing raw edges. The 2"/5cm-wide tape will turn into ½"/1.3cm-wide double-fold bias tape, and the 1½"/4cm-wide strip will turn into ⅜"/1cm-wide double-fold bias tape.

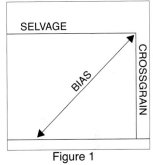

Figure 1

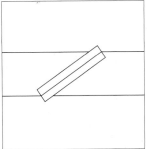

Figure 2

3 Trimming

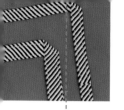

7 Untie skirt and lay flat on your working surface.

8 Pin the shorter ½"/1.3cm-wide bias tape along the hem of the skirt, 1"/2.5cm above the hem. Straight stitch along both edges of the bias tape, turning under raw edges.

9 Using water-soluble marking pen or tailor's chalk and ruler, map out placement lines for the bias tape pattern, starting 1"/2.5cm above the top of the stitched bias tape at one end of the skirt. Draw a 3½"/9cm line parallel to the bias tape, then draw a 4"/10cm line perpendicular to the previous line, running up the skirt. Next, draw another 3½"/9cm line at the top point of the 4"/10cm line, running parallel to the bias tape again, then draw another 4"/10cm line perpendicular to the bias tape, running back down toward the skirt hem, ending 1"/2.5cm above the bias tape. Repeat pattern along the skirt hem.

10 Using water-soluble marking pen or tailor's chalk and ruler, map out the second set of placement lines for the bias tape, with the second set beginning 1"/2.5cm above the first set of lines at one end of the skirt. Draw second set of placement lines mirroring the first set, extending them 1"/2.5cm beyond and above the first set of lines.

11 Pin longer strip of ½"/1.3cm-wide bias tape along the first set of placement lines, folding the tape at the corners and turning under raw edges; press [see illustration, right].

12 Straight stitch along both edges of the tape, securing it to the skirt.

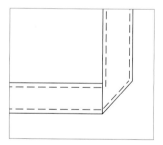

tip Clover has bias-tape folding tools in various widths that make creating your own bias tape a breeze. The tool creates single-fold bias tape, so when making double-folded tape, be sure to purchase a tool that is twice your finished width and simply press the tape in half.

13 Pin the longer strip of ⅜"/1cm-wide bias tape along the second set of placement lines, folding the tape at the corners and turning under raw edges; press.

14 Straight stitch along both edges of the tape, securing it to the skirt.

15 Pin remaining ⅜"/1cm-wide strip of bias tape along the edges of the pockets and across the waistband, turning under raw edges, and press.

16 Straight stitch along both edges of the tape, securing it to the skirt.

4 BEADING

GETTING STARTED

Basic supplies

- Beading needles
- Beads
- Thread (beading thread, clear nylon thread, etc.)
- Embroidery hoop (when applicable)
- Stabilizer (when applicable)
- Water-soluble marking pen
- Small round or oval jumprings
- Two chain-nose pliers

Commonly Used Bead Embroidery Techniques

Two embroidery stitches that you are now familiar with, running stitch and backstitch, are also used to secure beads to fabric.

1 Running stitch

Used to stitch one bead at a time to fabric [see illustration, right].

- Bring threaded beading needle up from wrong side of fabric.
- Slide one bead onto needle and into place where needle has emerged from right side of fabric.
- Reinsert needle into fabric at the edge of the bead, making a neat, tight stitch so you can barely see any thread on either side of the bead.
- Repeat steps 1–3, one bead/stitch at a time, for the length of the desired motif.

2 Backstitch

Used to stitch either one bead [Figure 1],
or several beads at a time [Figure 2].

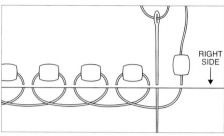

Figure 1

For single beads

• Bring needle up from wrong side of fabric.

• Slide one bead onto the thread and reinsert the
needle back through right side of fabric.

• Bring needle back up through the fabric one
bead's width away from the first bead.

• Slide one bead onto the thread and reinsert the needle back through the fabric right
next to the first bead. Pull thread taut.

• Repeat steps 3 and 4 for the length of the design.

For up to five beads per stitch

• Bring needle up from wrong side of fabric.

• Slide five beads onto thread and reinsert needle
back through right side of fabric.

• Come back up from wrong side of fabric
between second and third beads.

• Thread the needle through the three end beads.

• When the needle reemerges from the three
already-secured beads, add the next five beads.

• Reinsert needle and repeat steps 3–5 for the
length of the design.

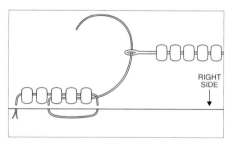

Figure 2

3 Couching

Used to stitch a strand of six or more beads [see illustration, right].

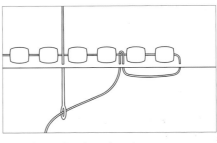

• Knot thread and pull up through fabric from the wrong side.

• String desired number of beads onto the thread.

• Lay into place on the right side of the fabric, then reinsert the needle at the end of the beads, being careful to keep the thread and beads taut.

• Come back up through the wrong side of the fabric, making a tiny stitch between two beads that secures the stranded thread to the fabric but is not visible when the beads slide back into place on top of it.

• Repeat step 4 between every third or fourth bead for the length of the strand.

Studio Sweater

EASY

Incredibly quick to bead, this rewarding project can be completed in less than an hour but leaves you with a strikingly chic finished product. Inspired by vintage Hollywood glamour, the radiating black sequins create a flattering halo to frame your face in picture-perfect elegance.

Supplies

- Crew-neck sweater or cardigan
- Thin-weight fusible interfacing
- 8mm flat sequins in black
- 10mm flat sequins in black
- 2mm to 3mm beads in black
- Hand-beading needle
- Black thread
- Water-soluble marking pen
- Scissors
- Ruler
- Iron

1 Turn sweater inside out. Following the manufacturer's directions, adhere fusible interfacing to the neck and upper chest area using a warm iron (or if fusible interfacing is not available, pin tear-away stabilizer into the same position).

2 Using water-soluble marking pen, make dots around sweater just outside the neck opening, approximately ½"/1.3cm from the neck and 1"/2.5cm to 1½"/4cm from each other.

3 Thread beading needle and knot at one end. Bring needle through the sweater from wrong side of fabric at first marked point. Thread a single 10mm sequin onto needle, followed by a single bead.

4 Reinsert needle back through hole in sequin [see illustration, right]. The bead will hold the sequin in place. Cut thread and knot on the wrong side of the sweater.

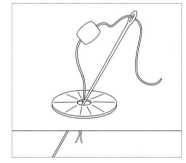

5 Repeat around neckline until last marked point has been beaded.

Studio Sweater

6 Using water-soluble marking pen and ruler, make a dot approximately 1"/2.5cm to 1½"/4cm below each black sequin. **Note** Take care to follow the natural curve of the neckline when marking points. Position the ruler perpendicular to the neckline in order to properly angle each point. The newly marked points should appear to radiate out from the curved neckline. If this is not the case, remove marks using a damp cloth and begin again.

7 Repeat step 6 to create a third ring of marked points, once again being careful to follow the curve of the neckline.

8 Repeat steps 3 and 4 at all marked points to create a second row of sequins, this time using the 8mm size.

9 Use black seed beads without any sequins for the third marked row.

tip A fourth ring may also be added using black seed beads. For an even more dramatic effect, especially if using a cardigan sweater, continue the beading all the way around the back of the neckline.

Patina Heirloom Purse

MODERATE

Infused with Art Nouveau elegance, this bag is created using simple bead-stringing techniques. You can source your medallion from antique shops, flea markets, your grandma's costume jewelry collection, or a jewelry supply company. The search for the perfect medallion is half the fun of making this one-of-a-kind purse!

Supplies

- New or vintage purse with straight, flat metal frame
- Sturdy upholstery gimp with a looped edge, hot glue gun and hot glue sticks [see note]
- 3mm glass beads in white
- 4mm to 7mm graduated glass beads in white
- Four 16 x 11mm frosted glass teardrop beads in green

- Three 8 x 6mm gold-plated oval jumprings
- Four 5mm gold-plated round jumprings
- Two chain-nosed pliers
- Metal medallion in bronze or copper
- Green patina solution
- Beading needle

- Beading thread
- Hand-sewing needle
- Thread
- Small plastic container
- Waxed paper
- Beading tray
- Latex gloves

Prepare bag for attaching beads

Note For the purse shown here, the existing metal detailing was used to attach medallion and beads. If your purse doesn't have this feature, add a strip of gimp as follows:

1 Cut a piece of gimp to the same measurement as the width of the metal frame, plus ½"/1.3cm extra at each end.

2 Turn under ½"/1.3cm at each end and secure with several invisible stitches.

3 Hot-glue gimp to metal frame, making sure that the looped edge hangs down.

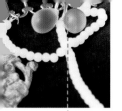

Prepare medallion

Note Always wear gloves when working with patina solutions. The metal piece used must be either copper or bronze, and must be free of rust and dust in order to achieve the patina effect.

1 Pour patina solution into a shallow plastic container. Dip or immerse medallion into solution following the manufacturer's directions.

2 Allow to dry completely overnight on a sheet of waxed paper.

3 Repeat steps 1 and 2 to increase patina effect if desired.

Attach decorations with jumprings

Attach medallion and beads using jumprings. To open a jumpring, hold each side of the jumpring using a chain-nose plier. Twist one plier away from you, thread jumpring onto a gimp loop, then close the jumpring by twisting the same side of the jumpring toward you. There should be no gap between the ends of the jumpring. **Note** Do not bend the jumpring open because it's nearly impossible to bend it back to where there is no large gap between the ends. Twisting the ring open instead will help to avoid this problem.

tip When using beads that have been purchased on strands of cotton thread, a time-saving technique is to tape one end of the purchased thread strand to a countertop. Then thread beading needle onto a new length of thread and lift the loose end of the purchased thread strand to pull it taught. Run needle through the beads, pulling five to eight beads at a time onto beading thread. This tip is particularly useful when the stranded beads are graduated in size.

Prepare beaded strands

1 For the long strand of beads, knot beading thread to an oval jumpring at one end and thread the other end onto a beading needle. Thread 14"/35.5cm worth of white glass beads onto the thread, beginning with 3mm beads then gradually increasing in size to a 7mm bead at the 7"/17.5cm mark (use the measurement guidelines on beading tray to center the 7mm bead) before decreasing gradually to 3mm beads again. Knot end of thread to another oval jumpring.

2 Using the extra lengths of thread hanging at the end of each strand, thread two green glass teardrop beads to the base of the jumpring where the ends of the strand are attached. Knot securely. **Note** When tying off beaded strands, it is always best to leave a few millimeters of space to form slack rather than pulling the thread tightly before knotting. This allows the beads to drape.

3 For the two short strands, knot a strand of beading thread to a round jumpring with the other end threaded onto a beading needle. Thread 3½"/9cm of 3mm beads onto the thread. Knot a round jumpring at the other end. Repeat to form a second identical strand.

Decorate purse

Attach the medallion to center gimp (or metal) loop using an oval jumpring. Using its jumprings, attach each end of the long beaded strand approximately 1½"/4cm from the medallion jumpring. Using its jumprings, attach each end of a short beaded strand approximately ½"/1.3cm from a long strand jumpring. Repeat for remaining short beaded strand.

Cabaret Beaded Blouse

INVOLVED

This project completely demystifies hand-beading. Rather than fussing with a complicated image transfer, simply choose a blouse that features a floral print, raised embroidery design or cutwork motif, then add beading to enhance the existing design. Monochromatic seed beads, like we've chosen here, maximize sparkle but also keep the look polished instead of fussy.

Supplies

- Blouse
- Seed beads
- Thread
- Beading needle
- Embroidery hoop

1 Mount blouse in embroidery hoop with the area to be beaded inside of the hoop. Thread needle and knot one end.

2 To attach beads using a backstitch, bring needle up through wrong side of fabric to the right side of the blouse. Slide one bead onto the thread and reinsert the needle back through the blouse.

3 Bring needle back up through the fabric one bead's width of distance away from the first bead. Slide one bead onto the thread and reinsert the needle back through the fabric right next to the first bead. Pull thread taut.

4 Repeat step 3 to add beads along the blouse motif.

5 After the last bead, bring needle through the fabric to the wrong side of the blouse. Knot thread and trim away excess.

4 Beading

tip Instead of trying to bead an entire blouse, which could take a lifetime to complete, choose smaller details to accent with contrasting beads.

GETTING STARTED

Basic supplies

- 100 percent wool sweater(s)
- Washing machine and dryer
- Scissors or pinking shears
- Embroidery and/or sewing needles (where applicable)
- Thread or floss (where applicable)
- Clover Felting Tool
- Yardstick
- Tape measure
- Straight pins
- Paper-backed fusible webbing (where applicable)
- Rotary cutter and cutting mat (where applicable)
- Steamer or iron (where applicable)

How to felt wool

1 Make sure your sweater is 100 percent wool.

2 Machine wash on hottest setting OR bring to a boil on your stovetop in a 9-quart pot.

3 Machine dry on hottest setting (for at least one hour, if not more).

4 Repeat steps 2 and 3 until the wool becomes extremely dense and tight (should shrink to at least 30 percent smaller than original size, if not 50 percent or more). It may take up to three washing/dryings to fully felt a sweater.

Notes on cutting felted wool

• If felted sufficiently, your wool can be cut into desired shapes without unraveling, therefore making it unnecessary to finish any edges. If this is not the case, then the wool has not been sufficiently felted and should be washed/dried on hot settings again.

• For cutting strips of felted wool, a quilter's rotary cutter and mat can be used to ensure that each strip is uniform in width. **Note** Be very careful when using the rotary cutter, as the blade is extremely sharp. Always use a straightedge, preferably a thick metal yardstick, to make your cut, and keep your fingers as far away from the rotary blade as possible.

• Once cut, felted wool can be shaped somewhat using steam, which temporarily loosens the fibers. To shape the felted piece, steam using an iron or steamer, and a form that is held underneath the wool to create the shape. Hold the steam as close as possible to the felted wool (without burning your fingers), then pull and shape the dampened wool into place on your form.

• It is sometimes desirable to secure a grouping of felted wool elements together from the wrong side of the project. A recommended and effective method for doing so is to use paper-backed fusible webbing between the wrong side of the felted project and a piece of material for lining. This will make your felted project more durable, and more comfortable against the skin for those with mild wool allergies who may find direct contact with their skin a bit itchy.

Starboard Head Cozy

EASY

Perennially classic but not especially warm, the head scarf tends to remain banished during the blustery days of winter. This version is lined with cozy felt to keep your ears toasty when the cold winds blow. One recycled sweater yields several headbands, so these warmers make an inexpensive but wonderfully crowd-pleasing holiday gift.

Supplies

- One felted sweater
- ¼yd/.25m printed fabric
- 1yd/1m piping
- Thread
- Straight pins
- Water-soluble marking pen
- Fabric scissors
- Paper scissors
- Photocopier
- Iron
- Zipper foot
- Sewing machine

1 Felt sweater thoroughly.

2 Enlarge templates 200 percent on photocopier and cut out.

3 Pin large template onto printed fabric and mark perimeter with water-soluble marking pen. Cut fabric accordingly.

4 Cut piping in half to create two 18"/45.5cm lengths. Pin piping along both curved edges of the right side of the fabric with raw edges even. Using a zipper foot, machine-stitch piping to fabric piece along both curved sides close to the cord edges. Turn seam allowances to the wrong side and press. Set fabric piece aside.

5 Pin large template to felted sweater and cut accordingly. Pin small triangle template onto felted sweater and cut accordingly (two triangles will be needed to complete the project).

6 Center fabric piece on larger felted piece and pin down the center to hold in place.

7 Using the zipper foot, machine-sew single-stitch seams near edge of fabric piece so that seam goes through all three layers (fabric, piping and wool).

5 Felting

tip Winterize your favorite vintage scarf (it must be at least 6"/15cm x 12"/30.5cm) by using it for the contrast band instead of purchasing new fabric.

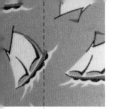

Starboard Head Cozy

8 Place wider ends of triangles over each end of the band, overlapping ¾"/2cm.

9 Machine-stitch triangle pieces to band using continuous stitch lines to create a rectangle of stitching that will securely hold the pieces together.

Farmer's Market Tote

MODERATE

This quick project uses panels of felted wool to transform a single recycled sweater into a sturdy yet style-savvy shopping tote. Inspired by vintage carpetbags, this handy accessory is large enough to handle anything from your current knitting project to the veggies for your evening meal.

Supplies

- One felted Fair Isle or striped sweater
- One pair 12½"/31.5cm-wide wooden handles
- Matching thread

- Embroidery floss in matching or contrasting color
- Embroidery needle
- Hand-sewing needle

- Straight pins
- Ruler
- Sewing machine

1 Felt sweater thoroughly.

2 Cut out the following panels from felted sweater: two 12½"/31.5cm x 11"/28cm (front and back panels), two 4"/10cm x 9½"/24cm (side panels) and one 12½"/31.5cm x 4"/10cm (bottom panel). **Note** If using a patterned or striped sweater, as shown, be careful to cut all panels so that stripes or pattern will match up on the front, back and side panels when they are sewn together.

3 Pin side panels to front and back panels with wrong sides together, raw edges even and matching bottom corners. **Note** There will be a notched area where the side panels are slightly shorter than the front and back panels—this is the extra length allowance necessary to attach the handles [see illustration, right].

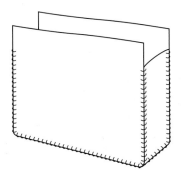

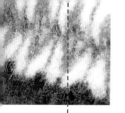

Farmer's Market Tote

4 Thread embroidery needle, knot at one end, and sew panels together using the blanket stitch. This stitch will produce a secure, even seam that can remain exposed to provide an additional decorative detail if a contrasting color floss is used.

5 Pin bottom panel to bottom edges of tote and sew together using the blanket stitch.

6 Once all pieces have been securely sewn together, slide the extra length at the top of the front and back panels through the opening at the bottom of each purse handle. Thread hand-sewing needle with matching thread and hand-stitch handles to tote using stitches that are barely visible on the outside of the tote.

tip In order to make the tote bag extra-sturdy, cut out a 12½"/31.5cm x 4"/10cm piece of heavy-duty corrugated cardboard to be placed in the bottom of the bag. To hold cardboard in place, use a hole punch to make several holes around the edge of the cardboard rectangle, then anchor to the bottom of the bag by stitching and tightly knotting through the felt at each hole.

Falling Leaves Wrap

INVOLVED

Bold and wonderfully whimsical, yet oh-so-easy to make, this no-sew scarf will make you feel like the fashionable embodiment of autumn! It's a fun way to recycle several old print and solid sweaters into one simple project that's sure to rake in compliments.

Supplies

- Three felted sweaters in coordinating autumn colors (one striped sweater if desired)
- ¼yd/.25m jersey knit fabric
- ¼yd/.25m Wonder Under

- for medium- to lightweight fabrics
- Clover Felting Tool
- Fabric scissors
- Paper scissors
- Heavy-duty craft scissors

- Tracing paper
- Cardboard
- Pen
- Washcloth
- Iron

Falling Leaves Wrap

1 Felt all sweaters thoroughly.

2 Trace leaf templates using tracing paper and pen. Make cardboard templates using traced leaf shapes.

3 Cut leaf shapes out of felted wool, using one shape per color. The smallest leaf pattern should be used for a dozen leaves from each sweater in addition to the larger leaves.

4 Lay out leaves (working a few inches/centimeters at a time) so that they overlap by at least ½"/1.3cm with several other leaves, being careful to allow no spaces between leaves whatsoever. **Note** It will be necessary to lay out the leaves as you construct the scarf, felting them together as you go and building a longer and longer scarf. It is best to keep the pattern approximately 6"/15cm wide—any wider and it will become difficult to wrap around your neck once completed.

5 Following manufacturer's directions, use Clover Felting Tool to felt leaves together by carefully laying the layered leaves onto the felting brush, right side up, and pounding with the needled felting tool. Once scarf has reached a length of approximately 36"/91.5cm, set it aside.

6 Lay jersey knit fabric out on work surface and cut one 8"/20.5cm x 40"/101.5cm strip, then cut a same-size strip from Wonder Under.

7 Following manufacturer's directions, lay Wonder Under on top of jersey fabric with the rough adhesive side touching the fabric. Iron without steam. Carefully peel away paper backing from Wonder Under, leaving adhesive behind on jersey.

8 Lay leaf scarf right side down on a hard, flat surface like a countertop (this will work better than a padded ironing board). Place jersey on top of leaf scarf so that all areas of scarf are completely covered. Make sure that the adhesive side of the jersey is touching the back of the scarf.

tip You can substitute geometric shapes for our leaf templates if you prefer to explore colorways outside the fall palette.

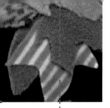

Falling Leaves Wrap

9 Following Wonder Under directions carefully, place a damp (not wet) washcloth on top of jersey fabric and press with iron on wool setting without steam. Make sure to press firmly and cover all leaf tips completely with iron, moving iron continuously to avoid scorching. Continue ironing process along the full length of the scarf, moistening washcloth as needed.

10 Allow scarf to cool and dry completely, then carefully trim away excess jersey from around the perimeter of the scarf.

11 If necessary, remoisten washcloth and reiron any leaf tips that remain loosely attached to the jersey fabric.

12 If desired, add a small button, a piece of Velcro, or a hook and eye to fasten scarf.

6 SILHOUETTE ALTERATIONS

GETTING STARTED

Basic supplies

- Tape measure
- Straight pins
- Tailor's chalk and/or water-soluble marking pen or marking pencil
- Dress form (if available)
- List of your personal measurements (including shoulders, bust, hips, waist and any other areas relevant to the particular project)
- Water-soluble fabric tape (where applicable)
- Sewing machine
- Hand-sewing needle
- Thread
- Fabric scissors
- Ruler
- Iron
- Ironing board

Commonly used silhouette alteration techniques

1 Pin-tucking

Typically appearing on blouses, pin-tucks both bring in (make smaller) the dimensions of a garment and add a decorative element. Most often, a thread color is chosen that matches the fabric of the garment, although thread in contrasting colors will make for a more dramatic effect. Pin-tucks are most easily achieved using a sewing machine. Begin by folding and pressing a straight line into place in the desired location for the pin-tuck, then use the machine to stitch a straight line along the folded edge. The amount of fabric being tucked will be determined by how far from the edge of the fold you choose to make your machine stitches, as well as the number of consecutive pin-tucks you plan to create side by side (as they are almost always done in groups). Most pin-tucks are very shallow (less than

¼"/.6cm), but they can be made much deeper if the garment must be taken in considerably. For example, an extra-large T-shirt can be resized to any dimensions by using properly placed, consecutive pin-tucks that are stitched as deep as 2"/5cm and then trimmed close to the stitching. For pin-tucks in one easy step, load your machine with a double-needle and pin-tuck foot (always check your machine's instruction manual). The double-needle pulls in the fabric to create flawless, ⅛" tucks and the foot is equipped with parallel grooves that help you align rows of pleats for perfectly placed tucks.

2 Hemming

Most often used to make minor alterations to a garment, hemming can also be used to completely change the look of a piece of clothing by transforming long sleeves to short, a maxi skirt to a mini, etc. Before creating a new hem, be certain to make accurate measurements and mark a guideline using your water-soluble marking pen or tailor's chalk in order to ensure a neat, straight edge.

You can finish your raw edges with bias tape or hem tape, or by folding it over twice and pressing in place. Press the hem allowance to the wrong side of the garment, and stitch the hem in place using your preferred sewing method. For some garments, a simple straight stitch with your machine will be appropriate, while for others, hand-sewing may be necessary so that your stitches will not be visible on the right side of the garment.

Tips for altering silhouettes

• Always mark new seams to be created with a water-soluble marking pen, marking pencil or tailor's chalk. Never begin to cut or sew without first marking your seam.

• Keeping your iron handy and warm is crucial. Always press a fold or a new edge under using your iron before you create the seam, then press again once the seam has been completed.

• When making drastic changes to a silhouette or a garment's size, it is particularly important to create basted seams before any final seams are made. This will enable you to ensure a proper fit or make any necessary adjustments before final seams have been created. There will often be a small adjustment to make, so this step will save you a tremendous amount of time in tearing out improperly placed seams.

Lily-Pad Skirt

EASY

Turn an A-line skirt from your closet's B-list into a swingy little number worthy of top fashion billing. A few crochet doilies, easily picked up at a flea market or thrift store, are quickly transformed into charming godets that are sure to add sashay to your step.

Supplies

- A-line skirt
- Crochet doilies or lace handkerchiefs
- Cut-away stabilizer
- Thread
- Water-soluble marking pen
- Temporary spray adhesive
- Fabric scissors
- Ruler
- Tape measure
- Fray Check
- Sewing machine

1 Determine how many godets are to be added to the skirt. Measure the circumference of the hem and divide by the number of godets to determine the space between them.

2 Using spray adhesive, adhere doilies to stabilizer. Cut each doily into uniformly sized wedges (each doily was cut into thirds for our example), cutting from the outer edge to the center point to form godets. Be careful not to separate the doily from the stabilizer while cutting.

3 Mark placements for the godets with a water-soluble marking pen, spacing them evenly around the hem of the skirt.

4 Measure the height of the godets and draw a line at each placement mark on the skirt equal to the godet height minus ½"/1.3cm, with the line perpendicular to the skirt hem.

5 Cut each line and press raw edges under ¼"/.6cm. Apply Fray Check at the top end of each slit.

6 Place one godet under one slit opening, overlapping the pressed edges of slit over cut edges of godet. Stitch ¼"/.6cm from each edge. Repeat for all godets.

7 Cut away stabilizer from the exposed doilies.

tip Instead of doilies, you can use any fabric or remnants to create contrasting godets. The heavier your fabric, the more it will affect the drape of your skirt, increasing the flared effect.

Crisp Cuffed Cutoffs

MODERATE

A simple way to salvage pants that are stained or torn, these preppy cuffed shorts elevate the style quotient far beyond the cutoff jeans of childhood. Choose a length that best flatters your figure, and finish with button tabs to give a more polished look.

Supplies

- Pants
- Two buttons
- Thread
- Pattern paper
- Water-soluble marking pen or tailor's chalk
- Scissors
- Pinking shears (optional)
- Ruler
- Tape measure
- Pen
- Sewing machine

Make cuffed shorts

1 Try on pants and mark the desired length of the shorts with water-soluble marking pen or tailor's chalk.

2 Using the ruler, mark a cut line ½"/1.3cm below the desired hemline on both legs. Measure the inseams and side seams of both pant legs with the tape measure to make sure that both pant legs will be cut identically. Cut around each leg.

3 Measure one leg front from side seam to inseam. On pattern paper, mark three parallel lines 1½"/4cm apart, the width of the front leg.

4 Extend center line ⅟₁₆"/.1cm on both ends. Draw a line from the ends of the center line to the ends of the top and bottom lines.

5 Add ½"/1.3cm seam allowances to the top, bottom and sides of the cuff pattern.

6 Repeat steps 3–5 to make back cuff pattern, measuring the back pant hem instead of the front.

7 Use patterns to cut two front cuffs and two back cuffs from the excess pants fabric.

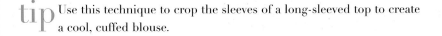

tip Use this technique to crop the sleeves of a long-sleeved top to create a cool, cuffed blouse.

Crisp Cuffed Cutoffs

8 Pin a front cuff to a back cuff with the right sides together and side edges even. Machine-stitch the side seams with a ½"/1.3cm seam allowance. Fold cuff in half with wrong sides together and raw edges matching. Press a crease into the cuff. Finish the raw edges of the cuff with a zigzag stitch or pinking shears. Make second cuff.

9 Open up one cuff and turn inside out. Pin the opened cuff to one pant leg with right sides together and raw edges even along one raw edge of the cuff, making sure that the side seams match up. Machine-stitch the cuff to bottom edge with a ½"/1.3cm seam allowance. Press seam allowance to the inside of the shorts.

10 Turn attached cuff down and fold the bottom half of it to the inside of the shorts at its original crease line. Match up the cuff's raw edges inside the shorts and pin in place. Hand-stitch the raw edges to the shorts using desired hemming technique.

11 Fold cuff up along the bottom hem and press in place.

12 Repeat steps 8–11 for second cuff.

Make button tabs

1 Enlarge button tab template [right] 200 percent and trace onto pattern paper. Cut out two tabs from excess pant legs.

2 Fold one tab in half with right sides together, matching points. Stitch around side and top raw edges using a ½"/1.3cm seam allowance. Clip the corners with scissors and turn right side out.

3 Trim the bottom edge with pinking shears or finish with a zigzag or overlock stitch.

4 Pin the finished tab to inside of each leg ½"/1.3cm inside the bottom hem of the shorts and centered on the side seam with raw edges even. Stitch. Fold tab up and pin to shorts above the cuff. Attach button to the shorts, sewing through tab to secure it to the shorts.

5 Repeat steps 2–4 for second tab.

Swing Blouse

INVOLVED

Inspired by the easy elegance and wearable silhouettes of 1940s sportswear, this blouse is ultra-feminine and extremely flattering thanks to artfully placed pin-tucks that accentuate the waistline. The subtly ruffled hemline created by the pin-tucks is an added bonus, completing an hourglass shape that conceals almost any flaw.

Supplies

- Unfitted blouse without darts in the front
- 1yd/1m of ½"/13mm-wide crushed velvet ribbon
- Thread
- Straight pins
- Water-soluble marking pen
- Ruler
- Sewing machine

1 Try on blouse and determine how much allowance needs to be taken up on one side of the front. Write down measurement.

2 Divide your measurement by ¼"/.6cm to determine how many ¼"/.6cm-deep pin-tucks will need to be made. The blouse shown needed to be taken in 2¼"/5.5cm on the front, and therefore needed nine pin-tucks.

3 Lay blouse flat on work surface and measure the width of the front-side piece, starting at the desired placement of the first pin-tuck and ending in the desired location of the last pin-tuck. Write down measurement and divide it by the number of pin-tucks determined in step 2 to find the amount of space between your pin-tucks. The front-side piece of the blouse shown is 9"/23cm wide, so the space between the pin-tucks is 1"/2.5cm.

4 With a water-soluble marking pen, draw pin-tuck placement lines parallel to the button placket and side seam, with the space between them being the amount determined in step 3. The blouse shown has nine parallel lines 1"/2.5cm apart. The tops of the pin tucks should be approximately 1½"/4cm below the bust point of the blouse, or 1½"/4cm below where the fullest part of the bust will be.

5 To stitch a pin-tuck at one placement line, fold blouse with wrong sides together with the crease along one placement line; pin in place. Stitch pin-tuck with a ⅛"/.3cm seam allowance with the crease being the edge of the seam allowance. Repeat for all pin-tucks.

6 Repeat steps 4 and 5 for other front side of the blouse [see illustration, right].

1/8"

7 With water-soluble marking pen, mark two placements on the back of the blouse for the ribbon at the waist of the shirt.

8 Cut velvet ribbon in half to make two 18"/45.5cm-long pieces.

9 Turn one edge of one piece of ribbon under ½"/1.3cm twice to encase raw edge. Machine- or hand-stitch ribbon, with the wrong side of the ribbon facing the right side of the blouse, at one placement mark on the back of the blouse. Be sure that the ribbon length is extended toward the center of the blouse.

10 Repeat step 9 for other piece of ribbon, attaching it to the other placement mark on the back of the blouse.

11 Remove all markings with water.

tip To highlight pin-tucks even more, stitch with a contrasting-color thread for standout stitch lines.

7 TECH-SAVVY TECHNIQUES

GETTING STARTED

Basic supplies

- Printable fabric (where applicable)

- Printable iron-on sheets (where applicable)

- Inkjet printable shrink plastic sheets (where applicable)

- Inkjet printer with color printing capability

- Digital or scanned images

- Iron and ironing board (where applicable)

Tips for successful tech-savvy crafting

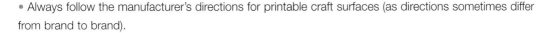

- Always follow the manufacturer's directions for printable craft surfaces (as directions sometimes differ from brand to brand).

- Do not attempt to use any of the printable craft surfaces with a laser or dot-matrix printer; they are appropriate for use with inkjet printers only, unless otherwise noted in the product's instructions.

- See Web resources list [back of book] for digital image resources.

- To ensure the best-quality image with saturated color, select the highest-quality photo setting on your printer.

- If you are creating an iron-on transfer and your image has text, mirror the image before printing so that the text will read correctly when ironed on.

- Don't limit yourself to just photos! If it can fit in your scanner bed, it can be scanned for your project.

- Printable iron-on image transfers work best with lighter-color shirts, as the color of the fabric will show through the image.

- When creating holes in a printable, shrinkable plastic design, punch holes in the plastic prior to shrinking. Attempting to drill holes after shrinking can cause cracks in the plastic.

- Since printable fabrics are now available in a variety of weaves and fiber contents, be sure to select the product that is appropriate for your project. For example, printable silk would not be sturdy enough to create the tote bag pocket featured in this chapter, and should be avoided in favor of more durable cotton.

Trompe L'Oeil Tee

EASY

Readily available iron-on paper for inkjet printers makes it possible to create your own custom T-shirt in less than thirty minutes. To recreate the trompe l'oeil effect show here, simply place an oversized bow directly on your scanner and capture the "3-D" image. A few clicks of the mouse later, you'll be ironing your way to a fashion-forward tee you won't see anywhere else.

Supplies

- T-shirt
- Wide ribbon, silk scarf or bowtie
- Iron-on image transfer paper for inkjet printers
- Computer
- Scanner
- Color inkjet printer
- Iron
- Craft scissors

1 To create image, tie a large bow using ribbon, silk scarf or bowtie (making sure it will fit on the scanner bed). Lay flat on scanner and create a digital image file using computer's scanner software.

2 Print image onto iron-on image transfer paper following manufacturer's directions. Allow to dry fully before touching image or attempting to cut out.

3 Using craft scissors, carefully cut out design.

4 Lay T-shirt flat on a hard surface such as a countertop (this will work better than a padded ironing board) and position iron-on with the image touching the fabric.

5 Following manufacturer's directions, adhere iron-on to T-shirt using iron.

6 Allow to cool completely, then carefully remove paper backing, making sure that entire image has adhered to shirt.

tip For another fun trompe l'oeil effect, try scanning vintage jewelry pieces, buttons or draped chains.

HAIRCUT and
OTHER STORIES
RING LARDNER
Preliminary
Mathematics
REVIEW
AMSCO
GUIDE
AN AMSCO SCHOOL PUBLICATION

Pocket-Edition Tote

MODERATE

Vintage paperback books with fabulous covers can be bought for pennies at yard sales, thrift shops and flea markets. Take advantage of the graphic possibilities with a pocket-front tote featuring your favorite finds on printable fabric. A quick and easy afternoon project, these handy satchels make a perfect gift for the bookworms in your life.

Supplies

- Tote bag
- Thread
- Seam ripper
- Water-soluble marking pen (optional)

- Ruler
- Two paperback books with interesting covers
- Printable (paper-backed) cotton twill fabric
- Computer

- Color inkjet printer
- Scanner
- Iron
- Sewing machine

1 Find two paperback books with interesting covers. (The books used in the example shown are high school textbooks from the early 1960s that were purchased for 50 cents each at a thrift store.) Scan book covers and rotate the images clockwise 90° so that the images are on their sides. Evenly space the images vertically (one above the other), in order to fit them both on one 8½"/21.5cm x 11"/28cm sheet of paper. **Note** This positioning can be done in Microsoft Word so that the page-size constraints will help to ensure proper sizing of the images.

2 Following manufacturer's directions, place one 8½"/21.5cm x 11"/28cm sheet of printable cotton twill fabric into paper tray and print using the highest-quality print setting available.

3 Follow manufacturer's directions for drying time, then remove the paper backing. This may include extra ironing steps or washing, so be sure to read directions carefully. Make sure the fabric has dried completely before moving to the next step.

Pocket-Edition Tote

4 Use seam ripper to open up sides of tote bag into one long, flat rectangle of fabric.

5 Fold over top edge of printed fabric approximately ½"/1.3cm and press. Machine-stitch a top hem.

6 Turn under sides and bottom of printable fabric pocket ½"/1.3cm and press.

7 Using tape measure, center printable fabric pocket on front of tote and mark location with pins or water-soluble marking pen. Pin pocket in place on front of tote using marked guidelines to ensure proper position.

8 Machine-stitch along each side and across bottom of printed fabric, leaving top open to create the pocket.

9 Turn tote inside out and restitch side seams, using original seam allowance.

10 Turn right side out and head to the library!

tip Printable fabric is available in many colors and fibers, including silk, cotton and linen. Every season craft companies introduce new variations on these products, which are perfect for self-cover buttons, appliqués and small home dec projects.

Fine-Art Halter

INVOLVED

A childhood favorite, shrink plastic sheets are all grown up thanks to a new inkjet-friendly variety. Scan your favorite postcard, go online to find free retro clip art, or mine the Internet for copyright-free imagery. We fell in love with this Art Nouveau advertisement, and it happened to match our recycled T-shirt perfectly.

Supplies

- Fitted T-shirt
- 1yd/1m of lingerie elastic with looped edge
- 2yd/2m of 2mm- or 3mm-wide ribbon
- Thread
- Straight pins
- Sewing machine
- Embroidery floss

- Embroidery needle
- Water-soluble marking pen
- Craft scissors
- Fabric scissors
- Color inkjet printer
- Computer
- Digital image
- Shrinkable plastic for inkjet printers

- Large bowl (for marking)
- Ruler
- Hole punch
- Aluminum foil or cookie sheet
- Oven
- Clear matte Krylon spray
- Needle threader (optional)

Fine-Art Halter

Prepare shrinkable plastic disc

1 Print desired image onto sheet of shrinkable plastic, following manufacturer's directions. **Note** Image should be at least 9½"/24cm to 10"/25.5cm wide and 6"/15cm to 8"/20.5cm tall, and should be oriented vertically to fit on one 8½"/21.5cm x 11"/28cm sheet. Allow ink to dry fully. Image will shrink to roughly one-third of its original size, so choose an image accordingly.

2 Using the edge of a large overturned bowl, mark a half-circle onto your image with permanent marker. Using a ruler, mark a straight line (the diameter) connecting the bottom points of the half-circle. **Note** The flat side should be no less than 8"/20.5cm, and the height of the half-circle should be no less than 6"/15cm at the central point.

3 Cut out design along the permanent marker guidelines.

4 Using hole punch, create evenly spaced consecutive holes across entire flat edge, as well as two sets of two adjacent holes at the two o'clock and ten o'clock positions on the half-circle (these will provide a place to thread the ribbon straps).

5 Shrink in oven following manufacturer's directions, letting cool completely before handling.

6 Apply one coat of clear matte Krylon spray to image side of disc. Allow to dry completely. Apply a second coat, letting dry for at least two hours before continuing with project.

Complete halter top

1 Lay T-shirt flat on a hard surface. **Note** Unless the preferred final product will be midriff-baring, choose a T-shirt that hits a few inches/centimeters below the beltline, as hem of finished halter will be 2"/5cm to 4"/10cm shorter than original T-shirt.

2 Place ruler on T-shirt directly under sleeves and use water-soluble marking pen to mark a cutting line just below the sleeve seams across the chest.

3 Pin both layers of the T-shirt together just below the cutting line. Cut along marked line through both layers, leaving only a tube of T-shirt with seams down each side.

4 Take personal measurements just above the bust (right below armpits) and all the way across the back. Cut the appropriate length of lingerie elastic to fit these measurements, subtracting 2"/5cm to 3"/7.5cm from measured length to allow the elastic to stretch around the body and hold the halter securely in place. Stitch short ends together, creating an elastic circle.

5 Pin elastic to top (cut) edge of T-shirt tube at four points: one at both side seams, one at center front and one at center back. Make sure that the looped edge of the elastic is positioned around the top edge of the tube so that the loops are free and not overlapping the jersey fabric.

6 Using sewing machine on the stretch straight-stitch setting (looks like a lightning bolt), stitch around entire elastic loop, stretching elastic between pinned points to keep elastic lined up evenly with T-shirt edge.

7 Thread embroidery needle with six strands of floss and thread through the first hole on the disc's flat edge. Knot in place.

8 Attach plastic disc to elastic loops using desired embroidery stitch, such as straight stitches perpendicular to disc, a variation on the blanket stitch (we used this in our example), or a series of crisscrossed single stitches that will give the appearance of X's along the disc's flat edge. Securely knot in place at final hole.

9 Cut ribbon into two 1yd/1m lengths. Thread one length of ribbon through each set of holes at the top of the disc (using a needle threader, if necessary, to pull the ribbon through). The ribbons should be long enough to tie in a bow at the back of the neck.

tip Printable shrink plastic can also be made into brooches, zipper pulls, graphic jewelry and other accessory projects.

8 DECONSTRUCTION/RECONSTRUCTION

GETTING STARTED

Basic supplies

- Tape measure
- Water-soluble marking pen or marking pencil (or tailor's chalk)
- Water-soluble fabric basting tape
- Straight pins
- Dress form (if available)
- Fabric scissors
- Sewing machine
- Straightedge ruler
- Iron
- Ironing board

Tips for successful deconstruction/reconstruction projects

• Always baste and try on the garment before making any final seams with the machine.

• Keep your iron hot and press each seam as you go. Often, pressing basted seams before the final pass can make the machine-sewing quicker and easier.

• If you want to combine two garments, first lay them both flat, one on top of the other, to determine if the important measurements of the two garments match up (such as shoulders, bust, waist, hips, etc.). If they differ in size, make the necessary alterations in size or shape before you proceed with the project by attempting to put elements of the two pieces together. This step will save you much time and frustration in the long run, and will ensure that your project comes out with even, smooth seams and a good fit.

Central Park Pants

EASY

Making gauchos is a fun way to reconstruct wide-legged pants into a more fashion-forward shape. Plus, the excess fabric you remove can be transformed into a pair of matching suspenders! Try altering wide-legged jeans for a year-round alternative to these summer whites.

Supplies

- White, wide-legged pants
- Four buttons to cover
- Contrast fabric to cover buttons
- Thread
- Hand-sewing needle
- Safety pin
- Water-soluble marking pen or tailor's chalk
- Fabric scissors
- Ruler
- Measuring tape
- Iron
- Sewing machine

Crop the pants

1 Try on pants and mark desired length of shorts with water-soluble marking pen or tailor's chalk.

2 Using the ruler, mark a cut line 1½"/4cm below the desired hemline on both legs. Measure up from the pant hem at the inseam and side seam on both pant legs with the tape measure to make sure that both legs will be cut identically. Cut around each leg.

3 Fold pants up at their new hemline and press in place. Hem pants using desired hemming technique.

Make the suspenders

1 Try on gauchos. Using the measuring tape, determine the length of the suspenders needed and mark button placements with the water-soluble marking pen.

2 Cut several 3½"/9cm-wide strips from the leftover white pants fabric. Stitch strips together with right sides together and short edges even to form one long strip that is the length of the suspender needed plus 1"/2.5cm. Press seams open.

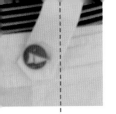

Central Park Pants

3 Fold strip in half with right sides facing and long edges even and pin together. Machine-stitch through both layers along the long edge of the strip with a ¼"/.6cm seam allowance to form the suspender.

4 Trim seam allowance to ⅛"/.3cm. Attach the safety pin to one end of the suspender. To turn suspender right side out, push the safety pin to the inside of the suspender and push it through to the other end. Remove the safety pin and press.

5 At one end of the stitched strip, push raw edges to the inside, forming a point. Pin and press in place. Repeat for the other end of the strip.

6 Machine-stitch a straight stitch around all the edges of the suspender, close to the edges.

7 Repeat steps 2–6 to make second suspender.

8 Following manufacturer's directions, cover buttons with contrasting fabric, centering desired motif on the button.

9 Using water-soluble marking pen, mark the placement of the buttonholes on the suspenders. The buttonholes should be ⅛"/.3cm larger than the diameter of the buttons.

10 Following manufacturer's directions, machine-stitch buttonholes onto the suspenders.

11 Hand-sew buttons at their marked placements on the gauchos, and remove any markings with water.

12 Attach suspenders to pants with the buttons.

tip If your pants have contrasting stitching or specialty seams like the pants shown here, try repeating them in the suspenders for a uniform look.

Victorian Tee

MODERATE

Easy to salvage from thrift stores, rummage sales or vintage shops, high-necked dresses with lace yokes were an omnipresent fashion staple of the 1980s. Converted from dowdy to downright fabulous when attached to a simple T-shirt, the lace collars can be found in a wide variety of colors and shapes to suit any taste. The finished effect is part Victorian lady and part Vivienne Westwood: unforced and effortlessly cool.

Supplies

- T-shirt
- Lace collar
- Thread
- Hand-sewing needle
- Straight pins
- Fabric scissors
- Seam ripper
- Sewing machine

Victorian Tee

1 Using the seam ripper or scissors, remove lace collar from salvaged blouse or dress, being careful not to damage the lace.

2 Lay T-shirt flat and slide collar onto T-shirt so that shoulder seams of collar line up with shoulder seams of T-shirt. Pin collar to T-shirt.

3 Baste collar to shirt.

4 Try on T-shirt to ensure that collar is positioned properly. It should be straight and centered, and should line up along shoulder seams. There should be no puckering of either the T-shirt or the collar, as both should be flat and smooth around entire basted seam.

5 Using a straight-stitch setting, use sewing machine to make a single, continuous seam, attaching collar to T-shirt. The seam should be made as closely as possible to the outer rim of the collar without allowing the stitches to become too visible. Remove basted stitches.

6 Turn inside out, then cut T-shirt neck away using fabric scissors, trimming the jersey fabric to ½"/1.3cm to ¼"/.6cm away from the seam you've just sewn. Discard neck.

7 Turn T-shirt right side out.

8 If desired, trim sleeves to remove their hem and create a more feminine cap-sleeved effect, as shown.

tip For larger bust sizes, put on the T-shirt, then pin the collar in place. This will compensate for the lack of stretch in the collar and ensure a perfect fit.

Bits-n-Pieces Blouse

INVOLVED

With a little help from your sewing machine, you can combine any two blouses to create the eclectic yet chic effect seen in this project. Choose the best elements to showcase from each blouse, and piece them together into your own little fashion masterpiece.

Supplies

- Two blouses that are very similar in size (or that have already been altered to be similar in size)
- Thread
- Hand-sewing needle
- Straight pins
- Tape measure
- Water-soluble marking pen or white marking pencil
- Dress form (or friend to help you fit blouse to yourself)
- Iron
- Sewing machine

1 Decide which blouse will be the base blouse and which will be used to supply certain key elements.

2 Set aside "base blouse" and lay "elements blouse" flat, determining which details will be incorporated into the final piece. (In the finished fashion shown here, the elements blouse contributed the ruffled collar, sleeve cuffs and front panel with curved top seam, ruffled hem, button placket and tie-back straps.)

3 Using fabric scissors, cut each of the chosen elements away from the rest of the blouse, being careful to leave a 1"/2.5cm seam allowance around all perimeters. **Note** It is easiest to select elements that are already bordered by an existing seam, which you will rely upon as a guideline when combining with base blouse. The 1"/2.5cm seam allowance should be measured outside these existing seams.

4 Turn under extra seam allowances for each element and press using the appropriate iron setting for the fabric content of the blouse.

5 Put base blouse on dress form, or try it on. With the help of a friend, if necessary, pin each element onto the base blouse in the proper position. Remove base blouse.

Bits-n-Pieces Blouse

6 Baste each element into place exactly along the fold line where the new seam will be created. Remove pins.

7 Press all basted seams. Try the blouse on to ensure that the fit has not been adversely affected and that all seams line up properly. The new elements must be properly placed in the appropriate locations on the base blouse.

8 Using sewing machine, make straight seams along all basted stitch lines to secure each element onto the base blouse. **Note** Remember that these seams should be sewn on the wrong side of the garment so that only the transition from one fabric to another is visible on the right side of the finished blouse.

9 Press all new seams flat from the right side of the blouse.

10 Cut away any unnecessary parts of the base blouse that are now hidden by the new elements (in the example shown, the collar, cuffs and fabric from behind the front panel were all removed). Trim away the excess fabric from the 1"/2.5cm seam allowance so that only ¼"/6mm of fabric remains along the inner seam.

tip For added flourish, add decorative piping at the seams where the two blouses are stitched together.

9 SURFACE MANIPULATION

GETTING STARTED

Basic supplies

- Fiber Etch
- Iron
- Rubber stamps
- Yarn
- Felting tool
- Water-soluble marking pen or tailor's chalk
- Spray bottle

Basic surface manipulation techniques

• Always check the fiber content of the garment to be altered. Certain techniques are restricted to 100 percent natural fibers, so be sure to double-check the manufacturer's directions on any product you use. For example, Fiber Etch will only work properly when applied to cellulosic materials such as cotton, linen or rayon.

• Fiber Etch works especially well on 100 percent cotton jersey fabrics. The woven knit will resist fraying around the edges of the burnout motif. Loosely woven fabrics that easily fray, such as traditional linens or cotton batistes, can be treated with a seam sealant like Dritz Fray-Check to prevent any unwanted raveling. Just remember to apply the Fray-Check after completely finishing the burnout process.

• Applying Fiber Etch to both sides of thicker fabrics such as denim will help ensure a successful burnout design.

• When choosing a velvet garment to emboss, keep in mind that longer piles tend to emboss more easily than shorter ones. Velvet blends containing rayon work best (polyesters will not perform as well when pressed). Clearly embossed images may prove difficult or impossible to achieve with newer stretch velvets, so stick to traditional velvet fabrics that will always yield the most desirable results.

• When embossing velvet, press for a maximum of approximately nine or ten seconds, but don't be afraid to use some muscle to apply pressure on the stamp. Rubber stamps are manufactured under high temperature conditions so they can handle the heat. If you need to press longer, simply lift the iron, reposition it and press again.

• If you can't find a design that suits your fancy at your local craft store, you can always have a stamp made with an original drawing, text in any font, or a clip art image. Many Web sites and stores such as www.rubbertrouble.com will inexpensively produce a stamp using whatever image you choose. You can even make your own from scratch using a Speedball Linoleum Cutter carving tool and Speedball Speedy Cut carvable block.

• When felting, test several different types of yarn to guarantee the desired final result. You may be surprised how some yarns look once they have been felted, so never skip this step.

Starry Night Tunic

EASY

Creating your own eyelet pattern is a breeze with new products that eat away natural fibers. Here, eyelets adorn the neckline of a black jersey tunic, but you can achieve the same effect on a much grander scale. Just remember to work in a well-ventilated area or near an open window.

Supplies

- 100% cotton, rayon or linen tunic
- Water-soluble marking pen or white marking pencil
- Fiber Etch
- Pencil with new eraser
- Newspaper or other scrap paper
- Iron
- Blow dryer (optional)

1 Iron area where eyelets will be created to remove any wrinkles.

2 Mark tiny dots on fabric using water-soluble marking pen or white marking pencil in desired eyelet pattern.

3 Slip newspaper between layers of fabric to ensure that Fiber Etch does not seep through to other side of garment.

4 Dip end of pencil eraser into Fiber Etch and touch to fabric at premarked locations. Dip eraser into gel between each dot, applying to each dot twice if necessary to transfer sufficient gel from tip of eraser to fabric.

5 Allow gel to dry completely, gently blowing with a warm blow dryer to speed up the process if desired.

6 Iron with a warm iron on the reverse (non-gelled) side of the fabric until a color change (usually to a brownish hue) is evident in each eyelet's position.

7 Hold fabric under cold running water until all etched fabric has washed away, leaving open eyelets in the predetermined pattern. Allow fabric to dry completely.

8 If desired, turn garment over and repeat steps 1–8 to continue eyelet motif on back of shoulders.

tip Fiber Etch will not work on polyester or many other synthetics (check the manufacturer's directions for details). To prevent fraying, stitch the outline of designs with contrasting polyester thread before applying Fiber Etch inside the stitch lines.

Belted Beatnik Top

MODERATE

Today's gorgeous fashion yarns aren't just for knitting! Here a black mock-turtleneck goes from stodgy to stunning with the help of novelty yarns and a silk ribbon belt. Simply add color and texture, as shown here, or create your own allover surface design.

Supplies

- Knit top
- 2yd/2m each of three contrasting novelty yarns
- 2yd/2m ribbon
- Matching thread
- Clover Felting Tool
- Water-soluble marking pen or tailor's chalk
- Sewing machine

1 Using water-soluble marking pen or tailor's chalk, mark desired design onto the top.

2 Following the manufacturer's directions for Clover Felting Tool, lightly felt the yarn onto the top along the marked placement lines. **Note** One of the yarns shown here is a ribbon, which can't be felted and must be stitched in place.

3 Topstitch yarns using a zigzag stitch to secure them to the top.

4 Cut two pieces of ribbon 2"/5cm long. Try on the T-shirt and mark where your waist is. Remove the T-shirt and sew a piece of ribbon to each side seam at the waist marking to create belt loops, making certain to turn under each end before stitching to ensure finished edges.

5 Slip the remaining length of ribbon through each belt loop and tie together in front.

tip Experiment with felting your yarns on scrap fabric first, if available, layering various yarns and felting at different intensities. For a completely different look, try placing yarn on the underside of the garment, then felt using the Clover tool to pull only a few fibers through to the right side.

Poet's Society Dress

INVOLVED

You can emboss any design your heart desires when you make your own stamp from scratch. Here, a simple lace-inspired motif complements the elegantly tailored lines of a velvet dress to add even more ladylike sophistication. If you prefer a more bohemian look, make several different stamps or repeat one design across the entire surface of the fabric.

Supplies

- Velvet dress or jumper
- Speedball Linoleum Cutter carving tool
- Speedball Speedy Cut 2¾ x 4½"/7 x 11.5cm carvable block
- Photocopier
- Transfer paper
- Pencil
- Water-soluble marking pen
- Ruler
- Seam ripper
- Hand-sewing needle
- Thread
- Spray bottle with water
- Iron

1 Copy template on a photocopier. Using transfer paper and pencil, transfer design to the surface of the linoleum block. Following manufacturer's directions, carve the outline of design into the block using the carving tool, then remove the background of the design until it's recessed ¼"/.6cm.

2 Remove the stitches from the hem of the dress using the seam ripper.

3 Turn dress inside out. Draw a line using the ruler and fabric marker on the wrong side of the dress at the desired bottom edge of your motif. Make marks along the line every 3½"/9cm to mark the sides of each design. Mark another line parallel to and 1½"/4cm above the first line. Mark every 3½"/9cm on the second line to mark the placement of the motifs, offsetting the design so the end of each motif lines up with the center of a motif on the first row.

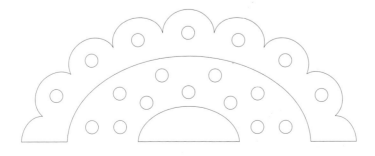

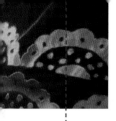

Poet's Society Dress

4 Place stamp inside the dress, with the rubber stamp pressed against the velvet nap and its edges even with the placement marks.

5 When the stamp is in position, spray the wrong side of the velvet with water to dampen the velvet. Preheat iron on wool setting. Holding the velvet securely, press the velvet over the stamp with the iron, being careful not to shift the fabric or the stamp. Hold iron in place for approximately 9–10 seconds. Lift iron, spray with water again and press iron on the stamp at a different angle to prevent leaving any impression of the steam holes. Hold iron in place for 9–10 seconds. Lift the iron. The stamp design should be vaguely visible on the wrong side of the velvet.

6 Repeat steps 4 and 5 for all marked placements of the stamp.

7 Hand-sew the hem of the dress.

tip If working on a particularly dark velvet, you may find it helpful to mark the desired placements of the motifs using tailor's chalk or by using a few small running stitches with contrasting thread.

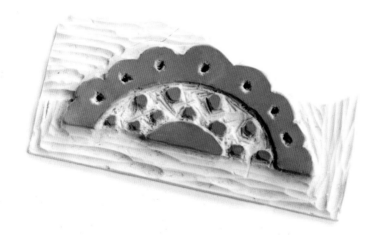

10 COLOR METHODS

GETTING STARTED

Basic supplies

- Silk dye
- Bleach pen
- Household bleach
- Fabric paint
- Potato
- Paring knife
- Paper scissors or craft knife
- Water-soluble marking pen or marking pencil
- Rubber or latex gloves
- Lightweight cardboard
- Ball-point pen or pencil for making designs on cardboard
- Iron or steamer (where applicable)
- Newspapers

Tips for successful color-method projects

• Use steam to set your silk dye. If using a steam iron, hang the garment rather than laying it flat, fill the water reservoir in your iron and turn it to the highest steam setting, then hold the iron about 1"/2.5cm to 2"/5cm away from the fabric (slightly below the dyed area) so that the steam permeates the silk without spitting droplets of water onto it. If droplets of water are allowed to make contact with the dyed portion of the silk, they will cause spotting and inconsistencies in the dye that will ruin the look of the finished project.

• Be very careful when washing off the gel from bleach-pen projects, as flecks of bleach can cause unwanted spots on the fabric. It is best to let the bleach-gel dry completely on the surface of the fabric before attempting to wash it off. That way it can simply be cracked and nudged away with your fingernail as the water runs over it, and the dried flecks of gel will not remove color from the surrounding fabric as they wash away.

• Another wonderful way to use bleach for color-method projects is a spray technique, ideal for dark-color garments made of natural fibers like cotton. First, prepare your work-space by placing newspaper over all nearby surfaces (you may want to do this outside if you have an appropriate area available). Lay your garment on a flat surface, then carefully place the elements of your decorative motif on top of the fabric. You can use leaves, shapes cut out of cardboard, pieces of lace, antique keys, different-sized buttons, etc.; just remember that anything you choose is about to be sprayed with bleach, so it must either be disposable or easily washed off. Wearing gloves, mix a bleach solution of one part bleach to one part water and pour into a spray bottle. Spritz the fabric, being careful not to disturb the objects you have placed on it. Allow the bleach to dry. After drying, immediately wash the fabric, by itself, in the washing machine. Machine- or line-dry, then press. Congratulations—you've just created your own original textile design!

Sailor-at-Heart Jacket

EASY

Inspired by the most popular maritime tattoo, the anchor motif on this denim jacket was created with nothing more than a bleach pen. This quick and easy project works best on darker denim, but if you don't have an appropriate jacket, don't fear—the anchors would look just as cute adorning the back pockets of your favorite denim jeans or skirt.

Supplies

- Dark denim jacket (or any other garment or accessory made from dark denim or canvas)
- Clorox Bleach Pen
- Tracing paper
- Pen
- Cardboard
- Craft scissors
- White water-soluble marking pencil
- Newspaper
- Safety pin
- Photocopier (optional)

1 Trace anchor template (first resizing with photocopier if desired), then cut out a cardboard template using the traced image.

2 Lay jacket on a hard, flat surface. Place the cardboard template in the desired position, then use white marking pencil to outline anchor shape onto denim.

3 Place several layers of newspaper between area to be bleached and back of jacket.

4 Being careful not to get any bleach gel outside the marked area, slowly fill in the anchor shape with a thick, even coat of bleach gel. **Note** To improve the finished effect, use a safety pin to pop any bubbles and smooth any inconsistent areas in the gel.

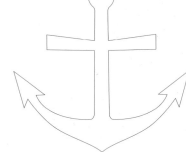

5 Allow bleach gel to dry completely (about forty-five minutes to one hour). When fully dry, it will appear crusty rather than moist and will be veined with small cracks throughout.

6 Under tub faucet or kitchen sink, carefully rinse away crusted bleach gel, making certain to rinse bleach away thoroughly.

7 Allow to dry. Launder jacket if desired.

tip If you prefer a more subtle color change rather than fully bleached white, simply wash away the gel before it has completely dried. Use a swatch of the fabric to test a few different bleaching times to create the desired effect.

Ballet Petal Skirt

MODERATE

Simple and elegant in shades of pink, the hem of this delicate silk wrap skirt has been dipped in fuchsia dye. The uneven color and wavering edge of this beautiful border evokes the sweetness of rose petals and creates a breezy romantic look.

Supplies

- 100 percent silk skirt
- One 3.5oz bottle of Tinfix Design silk dye in #28 carmine rose (or other steam-set silk dye)
- Mason jar
- Distilled water
- Disposable plastic paint tray
- Latex gloves
- Steamer or iron with steam setting
- Pants hanger
- Yardstick and clothes-pins (for a wrap skirt)
- Newspaper or drop cloth

1 Secure skirt in pants hanger, making sure that the hemline is hanging fairly evenly across the bottom. **Note** This project is best done outside, since dye can permanently stain carpet or upholstery.

2 Pour silk dye into Mason jar, fill to top with distilled water, screw top on tightly and gently agitate to mix diluted dye solution fully.

3 Lay out newspaper or drop cloth to protect all surfaces in the area. Put on latex gloves. Pour diluted dye solution into disposable paint tray at the deeper reservoir end.

4 Taking care not to splash the dye onto the skirt, hold hanger above paint tray so that the bottom 2"/5cm to 3"/7.5cm of the skirt dips into the dye solution.

5 Continue to hold skirt with bottom 2"/5cm to 3"/7.5cm immersed until the dye has steadily wicked up another 2"/5cm to 3"/7.5cm onto the silk (around twenty to thirty minutes).

6 Hang skirt to dry, taking care to have newspaper or a drop cloth underneath to protect all surrounding surfaces. **Note** Do not attempt to dry outside if there is more than a slight wind—the motion may cause dyed areas to make contact with undyed areas, resulting in unwanted splotches.

7 If skirt is a wrap style, secure the length of the waist to the yardstick using clothespins, then secure yardstick to pants hanger. After skirt is completely dry, use steamer or steam-iron to set dye. **Note** During the steaming process, the dye will continue to creep up and feather out around the upper edge of the dye line.

tip For a bolder effect, try dipping in a lighter dye first, then dipping halfway with a darker color.

Disco Star Wrap Skirt

INVOLVED

A grade-school staple, the potato stamp makes a bold statement on this fun, edgy wrap skirt. Best suited to geometric shapes, stamping with a potato is ideal for creating mod and op-art motifs.

Supplies

- Wrap skirt
- Large russet or Idaho potato
- Paring knife
- Fabric paint in pink and black
- Paper plate
- ½"/1.3cm-wide flat paintbrush
- Small round paintbrush (optional)
- Newspaper or drop cloth
- Scrap paper
- Iron

1 Cut potato in half widthwise. **Note** Potato stamp must be used immediately, and should not be stored for later use.

2 Using the paring knife, first use tip to score the outline of the star shape, then cut away the background. With the other half of the potato, carve another star, then hollow out its center.

3 Cover workspace with newspaper or drop cloth. Lay skirt out flat.

4 Pour a small amount of fabric paint onto a paper plate. Using flat paintbrush, distribute an even coat of paint over surface of paper plate. Dip potato stamp into the paint, making sure that there is an even coat of paint on the stamp. **Note** It's a good idea to practice first on scrap paper before committing to stamping on the fabric.

5 Following the design shown, or as desired, press the potato stamp on the skirt in the desired location. Carefully lift up stamp to avoid smearing. Reapply paint to stamp for next and following stampings. For best results, stamp one color first and allow to dry completely before applying next color. Let second color dry.

6 Using the round paintbrush, touch up stars if necessary. Let paint dry overnight. Following paint label directions, heat-set paints to make them permanent.

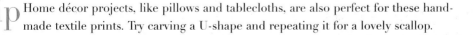 tip Home décor projects, like pillows and tablecloths, are also perfect for these hand-made textile prints. Try carving a U-shape and repeating it for a lovely scallop.

Here are terms to help you navigate the vast universe of textiles that is out there waiting for you.

acrylic Synthetic fiber with a soft, wool-like feel.

batiste Medium-weight plain-woven cotton or cotton blend.

bouclé Knit or woven fabric with a loopy knotted surface created by the texture of curly/knotted bouclé yarn.

broadcloth Plain tightly-woven cotton fabric.

brocade Heavy jacquard-type fabric featuring an allover pattern or floral design that is slightly raised.

calico Tightly woven cotton fabric with an allover print; typically a small floral against a contrasting background color.

chenille Yarn with protruding pile; usually made from wool, cotton, silk or rayon.

chiffon Very lightweight and sheer plain-weave fabric.

chintz Plain weave fabric glazed to produce a highly glossed and polished look.

corduroy Cotton with a cut and pile weave.

crinoline Plain weave stiffened fabric with a low yarn count.

damask Glossy jacquard featuring flat reversible patterns.

denim Twill weave cotton fabric made with different color warp and weft yarns (one color will predominate on the surface).

eyelet Fabric featuring patterned cut-outs often edged with stitching or embroidery detail to help prevent raveling.

felt Non-woven fabric made from fibers that are locked together using heat, moisture, and pressure to form a compacted material.

flannel Medium-weight plain or twill weave fabric that had been brushed on both sides to lift the fiber ends and create a soft surface effect.

gabardine Tightly woven twill worsted fabric with a slight diagonal grain line visible on the right side.

grosgrain Closely woven fabric, most commonly seen as a ribbon or trim, with narrow horizontal ribs.

herringbone Variation on the twill weave in which the twill grain is reversed at regular intervals, creating a zigzagged effect.

jacquard Any woven fabric that has been manufactured using the Jacquard attachment, which permits control of each individual warp yarn.

jersey Knit fabric with a smooth surface and more textured back side.

lamé Fabric woven using flat silver or gold metal threads to create either the design or the background of the fabric.

linen Fabric made from the fibers inside the woody stem of a flax plant (one of the oldest textile fibers).

muslin Inexpensive medium-weight plain weave sheeting fabric with a low thread count. Commonly used in fashion design for draping and making trial garments for fit purposes.

nylon Oldest completely synthetic textile fiber, widely used due to high durability and resilience.

ombre Color effect showing gradual changes from light to dark which is woven into the fabric by the arrangement of different toned warp threads.

organdy Stiffened sheer lightweight plain weave fabric with a crisp finish.

organza Crisp, sheer, lightweight plain weave fabric.

oxford Fine, soft, lightweight cotton or blended fabric featuring a 2 x 1 basket weave.

piqué A medium-weight knit or woven fabric, featuring raised designs such as cords, waffles, or other patterns.

polyester Synthetic fiber second only to cotton in common usage, featuring high strength, versatility, and low absorbency for quick drying.

rayon Manufactured fiber composed of regenerated cellulose (not a naturally occurring fiber, but a fiber composed of a naturally occurring substance).

satin Smooth fabric with a glossy face and a smooth back.

seersucker Woven fabric manufactured using modified tension control, resulting in a puckered stripe effect.

shantung Medium-weight plain weave fabric characterized by a textured semi-ribbed effect caused by slubbed yarns used in the warp direction.

silk Natural filament fiber produced by the silkworm in construction of its cocoon.

soutache Trim composed of a narrow braid in a herringbone pattern.

ruche Ruffled or gathered fabric or trim.

Spandex Elastomeric fiber that can withstand repeated stretching over 500% without breaking while still returning to its original length.

taffeta Crisp, smooth fabric with a slight sheen.

terrycloth Typical uncut pile-weave fabric.

tulle Lightweight, extremely fine machine-made netting, often featuring a hexagonal mesh effect.

velour Medium-weight closely woven fabric with a thick pile.

velvet Medium-weight cut-pile constructed fabric in which the cut pile stands up very straight.

velveteen Cotton cut-pile weave fabric with a much shorter pile than velvet.

viscose The most common variety of rayon.

voile Crisp lightweight plain-weave fabric with high-twist yarns in a very high thread count.

wool Usually associated with fibers or fabric from the fleece of a sheep or lamb, although any fabric constructed of animal hair may be termed wool.

The projects in this book give you a firm foundation in the skills you'll need to take control of your wardrobe and craft a look that is wonderfully, uniquely you. Now that you're ready to walk the *Fashion DIY* walk, we think you should be able to talk the talk as well. This list of fashion terminology gives you a comprehensive lesson in the language used by everyone from couture designers to home economics teachers to discuss garment construction and the elements of style.

a

A-line Dress or skirt resembling shape of an A.

appliqué (a-plee-kay) Fr. Motif applied to cloth or garment.

ascot Broad neck scarf; tied so that one end falls over the other.

asymmetrical One-sided, not geometrically balanced.

b

backing Fabric joined to wrong side of garment or garment area, typically for reinforcement or opacity.

backstitch Using the reverse-stitch function on the machine, stitch backwards and forwards in the same place to secure stitching.

band Strip used to hold, ornament or complete any part of garment or accessory.

baste Longer, temporary stitches. Used in gathering ruffles and set-in sleeve eases, as well as to temporarily hold two pieces of fabric together.

bateau Neckline following curve of collar-bone.

bell sleeve Full sleeve, flaring at lower edge like a bell.

bias Diagonal direction of fabric. True bias is at a 45° angle to grain lines.

binding Strip encasing edges as finish or trim.

bishop sleeve Sleeve that is full in the lower part, either loose or held by a band at wrist.

blind hem Hem sewn invisibly with hand stitches.

blouson Bloused effect of fullness gathered in at and falling over a seam, typically bodice over skirt.

bodice Portion of garment above the waist.

bolt Unit in which fabric is packaged and sold by manufacturer. Usually contains 12–20 yards/11–18 meters.

border Strip of self-fabric or commercial trimming used to finish edge.

c

cap sleeve Short sleeve just covering the shoulder and not continued under the arm.

cartridge pleat Rounded pleat that extends out rather than lying flat.

chevron V-shaped stripes.

chic (sheek) Fr. Originality and style in dress.

clip Cut in fabric to allow ease on curves or corners.

closure That which opens or closes a garment (buttons, zipper, etc.), or area on which they are placed.

colorfast Refers to fabric that will not fade or run during cleaning or laundering.

contrasting Opposing; showing off differences of color, fabric, shading, etc.

convertible Notched collar that can be worn either buttoned at neck or open with lapels.

couture (koo-tur) Fr. Sewing or needlework. Product of a seamstress; seam.

couturier (koo-too-ryay) m. or couturière (koo-too-ryare) f. Fr. Dressmaker; designer; head of a dressmaking house.

cowl Soft drape of fabric at neckline.

cravat Necktie folded or tied at front with ends tucked inside garment.

crew Round neckline that hugs the throat.

crosswise grain Threads that run across the width of the fabric and are perpendicular to the selvage.

cut-in-one Two or more sections cut in one piece, such as sleeve and bodice.

d

darts Folds used to take up excess fabric that taper to a point at either both or one end. Mainly used to shape garments over body curves.

décolleté (day-kawl-eh-tay) Fr. Cut low at neckline, exposing neck and back or cleavage of bosom as in formal evening dress.

dolman Sleeve set into a deep armhole so as to resemble a kimono sleeve.

double-breasted Front closing that overlaps enough to allow two rows of buttons.

dressmaking The art of sewing dresses, skirts, etc., as distinguished from tailoring.

drum lining Lining not sewn into garment seams.

e

edgestitch Topstitching placed very close to finished edge.

Edwardian Style of 1901–1910 when Edward VII was king of England.

empire Style of French Empire period; high waistline, décolleté, loose, straight skirt.

enclosed seams Concealed by two garment layers.

ensemble The entire costume. Usually, dress and coat.

epaulet Shoulder trimming, usually a band secured with a button.

epaulet sleeve Sleeve with square-cut shoulder section extending into neck in form of yoke. Also known as strap sleeve.

eyelet Small, round finished hole in garment or fabric.

f

face To finish an edge by applying a fitted piece of fabric, binding, etc. Also, the right side of the fabric.

faggoting Decorative stitch used to join two fabric sections that are spread apart.

fancy work Hand embroidery and needlework.

favoring Rolling one garment section slightly over another at the edge to conceal the seam.

finger press Pressing small area by creasing with fingers.

finish Any means of completing raw garment edge.

flap Shaped garment piece attached by only one edge.

flare Portion of garment that spreads out or widens.

fly Fabric used as lap to conceal opening in garment.

French curve A curved ruler often used to draw curved pattern pieces like armholes and necklines.

funnel collar Flaring outward at the top.

g

garni (gar-nee) Fr. Trimmed, garnished.

godet Triangular piece of cloth set into a garment for fullness or decoration.

gore Tapered section of garment; wider at lower edge.

grommet Large metal eyelet.

grosgrain Ribbon having heavy crosswise ribs.

gusset Fabric piece inserted at underarm to give ease in sleeve area.

h

halter Neckline having band around neck, attached to front of a backless bodice.

i

inset Fabric section or trim inserted within garment for fit or decoration.

interlining Layer of fabric between lining and underlining for warmth.

j

jabot Ruffle worn down front of bodice and fastened at neck.

jewel neck Simple, round neckline at base of neck.

k

keyhole Round neckline with inverted wedge-shaped opening at front.

kick pleat Pleat used for ease in a narrow skirt; may be a knife, inverted, or box pleat.

l

lantern sleeve Bell sleeve with wrist section joining at bottom, creating a shape resembling a lantern.

lap Any edge that extends over another edge, as on a placket.

lapels Part of garment that turns back, especially front part of garment that folds back to form continuation of collar.

layout Cutting chart on instruction sheet showing placement of pattern pieces.

lengthwise grain Threads that run parallel to the selvage of the fabric.

line Style, outline, or effect given by the cut and construction of the garment.

lingerie Women's lightweight underclothing.

m

macramé Knotted lace woven in geometrical patterns.

Mandarin Small standing collar that hugs neck.

mannequin (man-eh-kin) Fr. Dressmaker form, dummy. Person wearing new clothes to present at fashion show or collection.

marking Transfer of construction symbols from paper pattern to fabric.

martingale A half-belt or strap, generally placed on the back of a garment.

mini Hem length falling at mid-thigh.

miter Diagonal seaming at a corner.

mode (mowed) Fr. Fashion, manner, vogue.

motif Unit of design; used as decoration or pattern.

mounting Term sometimes used for underlining. Two layers of fabric are basted together and sewn as one.

n

nap Soft surface with fibers that lie smoothly in one direction.

notch (verb) Cutting wedges from seam allowances; (noun) pattern symbol transferred to fabrics to indicate matching points.

notions Items other than fabric or pattern required to complete garment.

o

opening Synonymous with closure; also, fashion showing of apparel for season.

p

peasant sleeve Full sleeve set into dropped shoulder and usually gathered into wristband.

pelt Skin of animal with fur intact.

peplum Small flounce or extension of garment around hips, usually from bodice.

peter pan Flat, shaped collar with round corners.

piece Specified length of goods as rolled from loom.

piece goods Fabric sold in pieces of fixed length or by the yard.

pin basting Pinning seams before stitching.

pinking Cutting raw edge with pinking or scalloping shears to retard raveling.

pivot Stitching around corner by leaving needle in fabric, raising presser foot, and turning fabric in new direction.

placket Garment opening fastened with zipper, snaps, buttons, or hooks and eyes.

plunge Neckline cut so low as to reveal curve of breasts.

prefold Folding and pressing garment section or binding before applying to garment.

preshape Shaping fabric into curves like those of area to which it will be applied; done with steam before stitching to garment.

preshrink Contracting fabric before construction.

prêt à porter (pret-ah-portay) Fr. Ready to wear.

princess line Garment fitted with seams instead of darts.

r

raw edge Unfinished edge of fabric.

remnant Unsold end of piece goods, leftover piece of cloth.

right side Finished side of fabric, outside of garment.

rip Removing stitches improperly placed; also, tearing fabric along straight grain.

roll Desired curve and fold (commonly on a collar); shaping established by pressing, pad stitching, etc.

s

sash Ornamental band or scarf worn around the body.

scalloped Cut into semicircles at edge or border.

scoop Deep neckline cut to shape of U.

seam allowance The width of fabric beyond seamline, not including garment area.

seam binding Ribbon-like tape used to finish edges.

secure Fasten permanently by means of knot, backstitching, etc.

self Of same material as rest of garment.

selvage Lengthwise finished edges on all woven fabrics.

semi-fitted Fitted to conform partly, but not too closely, to shape of figure.

shank Link between button and fabric to allow for thickness of overlapping fabric.

sheer Transparent fabric; comes in varying weights.

shrinking Contracting fabric with steam or water to eliminate excess in specific area.

silhouette Outline or contour of figure or garment.

single-breasted Center front closing with enough flap to allow one row of buttons.

slash Cut taken in fabric to facilitate construction.

slit Long, narrow opening; also, to cut lengthwise.

soft suit Dressy suit with a minimum of inner construction; also, dressmaker suit.

sportswear Garments meant for informal or casual wear.

stay Means of maintaining shape of garment area.

stiletto Pointed instrument for punching holes in fabric; smaller version called awl.

stitch in the ditch To hold two pieces of fabric together by straight-stitching in the well of the seam on the right side of a previously stitched seam.

surplice Bodice with one side wrapping over the other side.

t

tab Small flap or loop attached at one end.

tack Joining two garment layers with small, loose hand stitches or thread loop.

tailoring Construction technique requiring special hand-sewing and pressing to mold fabric into finished garment.

taper Cutting or stitching at slight diagonal, generally to make gradually smaller.

tension Amount of pull on thread or fabric during construction of garment.

thread count Number of threads in one square inch of fabric.

topstitching Machine stitching parallel to seam or edge, done from right side of garment.

transfer pattern Commercial pattern having design stamped on paper, usually transferred to fabric by iron.

trim To cut away excess fabric.

trimming Feature added to garment for ornamentation.

turnover A garment section, usually collar or cuff, which folds back upon itself.

turtleneck High turnover collar that hugs throat.

twill tape Firmly woven tape.

u

underlining Fabric joined in garment seams to give inner shape or support.

understitch Folding seam allowance to the facing or underside of the project and stitching close to the seam on the facing. Keeps the seam lying flat and the seam edge from showing from the right side.

v

V-neck Neckline shaped in front like the letter V.

vent Faced or lined slash in garment for ease.

w

welt Strip of material stitched to seam, border or edge.

wrap-around Garment or part of a garment wrapped around person, as for a cape or skirt.

wrong side Side of fabric on inside of garment.

y

yardage block Guide on back of pattern envelope; includes garment description, measurement, yardage, notions, etc.

yoke Fitted portion of garment, usually at shoulders or hips, designed to support rest of garment hanging from it.

Beaded Embellishment: Techniques & Designs for Embroidering on Cloth. Robin Atkins and Amy C. Clark, Interweave Press, 2002.

Beading on Fabric: Encyclopedia of Bead Stitch Techniques. Larkin Jean Van Horn, Interweave Press 2006.

Complete Guide to Embroidery Stitches: Photographs, Diagrams and Instructions for Over 260 Stitches. Ann-Marie Bakewell, Jennifer Campbell and Reader's Digest Editors, Reader's Digest, Inc., 2006.

Creative Surface Design: Painting, Stamping, Stenciling, and Embossing Fabric & More. Sandy Scrivano, Taunton Press, 2002.

The Embroidery Stitch Bible. Betty Barnden, Krause Publications, 2003.

Encyclopedia of Sewing Machine Techniques. Nancy Bednar, Sterling Publishing, 2001.

Handpainting Fabric: Easy, Elegant Techniques. Margaret Allyson and Michelle Newman, Watson-Guptill Publications, 2003.

More Fabric Savvy: A Quick Reference Guide to Selecting and Sewing Fabric. Sandra Betzina, Taunton Press, 2004.

Ribbonwork, the Complete Guide: Techniques for Making

Ribbon Flowers and Trimmings. Helen Gibb, Krause Publications, 2004.

Silk Ribbon Embroidery Bible: The Essential Illustrated Reference to Designs and Techniques. Joan Gordon, Krause Publications, 2005.

Sewing 101: A Beginner's Guide to Sewing. Editors of Creative Publishing International, Creative Publishing International, 2002.

Sew U: The Built By Wendy Guide to Making Your Own Wardrobe. Wendy Mullen, Bulfinch Press, 2006.

Sublime Stitching. Jenny Hart, Chronicle Books, 2006.

Tease: Inspired T-shirt Transformations by Superstars of Art, Craft, and Design. Sarah Sockit, Perigee Books, 2006.

The Complete Photo Guide to Sewing (Singer). Editors of Creative Publishing International, Creative Publishing International, 2005.

The New Appliqué: Innovative Techniques, Easy Projects. Trice Boerens and Kevin Dilley, Watson-Guptill Publications, 2004.

The Potter Needlework Library: Appliqué. Lucinda Ganderton, Potter Craft, 2006.

Vogue Sewing Revised and Updated. Sixth&Spring Books, 2006.

PROJECT RESOURCES

Secret Garden Skirt (page 26)
Bucilla 4mm and 7mm silk embroidery ribbon available from:
Crafts, Etc!
Attention Customer Service
7717 SW 44th Street
Oklahoma City, OK 73179
1-800-888-0321 ext. 1275
www.craftsetc.com

Studio Sweater (page 56)
8mm and 10mm flat sequins, and 2mm to 3mm beads available from:
Pearl Paint NYC Craft Center
42 Lispenard Street
New York, NY 10013
212-431-7932 ext. 3717

Patina Heirloom Handbag (page 60)
Upholstery gimp with looped edge available from:
www.rutherfordsdesign.com or call
877-427-0888
3mm and 4mm to 7mm graduated glass beads, and frosted glass teardrop

beads:
www.guidetobeadwork.com (for a store nearest you)
Bronze or copper metal medallion, and green patina solution available from:
Metalliferous, Inc.
34 West 46th Street
New York, NY 10036
888-944-0909
www.metalliferous.com
Beading needle, beading thread, and beading tray available from:
www.joann.com

Starboard Head Cozy (page 68),
Farmer's Market Tote (page 72) and
Falling Leaves Wrap (page 75)
Clover Felting Tool available from:
www.joann.com

Trompe L'Oeil Tee (page 92)
Iron-on image transfer paper for inkjet printers available from:
www.joann.com

Pocket-Edition Tote (page 94)
Printable (fabric backed) cotton twill fabric and computer available from:
www.hancockfabrics.com

Fine-Art Halter (page 97)
Shrinkable plastic for inkjet printers available from:
www.shrinkydinks.gomerchant7.com (for a store nearest you)
Krylon clear matte spray:
www.krylon.com (for a store nearest you)

Starry Night Tunic (page 114)
Fiber Etch available from:
Silkpaint Corporation
PO Box 18 INT
Waldron, MO 64092
800-563-0074
www.silkpaint.com
Fray Check available from:
www.hancockfabrics.com

Fabrics and notions

www.barkclothhawaii.com
Featuring a wide variety of barkcloth in retro, home dec, and floral designs.

www.denverfabrics.com
Featured fabric groupings include: apparel, bridal, dancewear, leather, oilcloth, outdoor, and vinyl. Also has appliqués, books, notions, patterns, and trims.

www.emmaonesock.com
Wide and ever-changing selection of designer fabrics in a variety of fibers including: knit prints, velvets, cotton woven prints, linen and hemp, sweater knits, rayon blend wovens and knits, silk wovens and knits, rayon/lycra jersey, jersey, silk prints, novelty and stretch laces, wool wovens and knits, and stretch linings.

www.fabric.com
Wide variety of fabrics for all uses and in all fibers, as well as notions, and patterns. Excellent prices.

www.fabricdame.com
Very cool designer fabrics with edgy prints. Decent prices, patterns, and notions as well.

www.fashionfabricsclub.com
Wide selection of designer fabrics in a variety of fibers including all major textile fibers, home dec fabrics, and indoor/outdoor yardage. Also has notions, trims, thread, and lining fabrics.

www.freespiritfabric.com
Featured designers: Sis Boom, Jane Davies, Jennifer Paganelli, Anna Maria Horner, Kristine Baerlin, and Denyse Schmidt.

www.hancockfabrics.com
One-stop shopping, good prices, and frequent deals on sewing machines.

www.joann.com
Sells everything you need at very competitive prices, with frequent sales.

www.kitty-craft.com
Amazing selection of fabrics (including a vast selection of outstanding retro prints and Japanese textile designer collections) in a variety of fibers and textures, such as linen, cotton, waffle-weave, herringbone weaves, jacquards, and twills. Plus, ribbons and trims, buttons, and some tools including the Clover Felting Tool.

www.michaelmillerfabrics.com
Extensive cotton print collections, fabric paper, and more.

www.pmorganics.com
Certified organic cotton fabrics, yarns, and notions.

www.purlsoho.com
Accessories & Notions page features fabric bundles which contain ½yd/.5m each of six or seven 100% cotton fabrics (enough to make a quilt top), and a decent list of sewing notions.

www.reprodepot.com
Trims, patterns, appliqués, patches, buttons, barkcloth, upholstery, extensive cotton broadcloth collections (including: 20's, 30's, 40's, 50's, 60's, 70's, kids, graphic design-y Japanese motifs, African influences, home dec and floral). Featured designers: Marimekko, Heather Ross, Amy Butler, Kaffe Fassett, and Denyse Schmidt.

www.rickrack.com
Authentic antique and vintage fabrics.

Resources and digital imagery

www.allbrands.com
Extensive selection of sewing machines, embroidery machines, irons, steamers, knitting machines, sergers, and sewing machine accessories.

www.craftster.org
Forums, DIY projects, blogs, classifieds, and picture hosting.

www.cutxpaste.com
Great links page, and opportunity to sell your DIY projects on a consignment basis.

www.getcrafty.com
Crafty columns, How-to's and DIY projects, great ideas, forums, blogs, and picture hosting.

www.lacis.com
Wide selection of purse frames/handles/hardware, needlework tools, hat forms, knitting notions, and books.

www.lindrix.com/textilelinks/fabriclinks
A huge listing of online fabric and sewing resources organized by fabric type.

www.makeworkshop.com
Offering craft and sewing classes year-round as well as a great links page.

www.missmary.com
Beautiful digital image collections from the Victorian era.

www.nypl.org/digital/index
Extensive searchable database of images, available for purchase but also fantastic to search for inspiration!

www.retrographix.com
Free retro clip art available for download. Perfect for creating embroidery templates or using on printable fabric, iron-on, or printable shrinky-dink.

www.sewfastseweasy.com
Selling sewing machines, sergers, patterns, notions, books, dress forms, etc., and offering sewing and knitting classes (both hands on for New Yorkers and online for everyone else).

www.sublimestitching.com
Embroidery templates, supplies and tools, inspiration, kits, and blanks (such as tea towels or pillow cases), as well as a customer gallery for displaying projects!

www.thevintageworkshop.com/store
Digital image collections as well as many inkjet printable materials: Cotton and poplin fabric sheets, fine art paper, vellum, iron-on transfer sheets, and more.

www.whatthecraft.com
Great tutorials for sewing basics, including good illustrations and figures to help make things clear. Features a slew of free project instructions, forums, good web resource lists, an excellent links page, super fun contests, and DIY challenges!

Notions and trims
www.denverfabrics.com

www.fabric.com

www.fashionfabricsclub.com

www.hancockfabrics.com

www.joann.com

www.metalliferous.com
Seemingly endless variety of metal jewelry components and findings, and all supplies and tools needed for metal jewelry crafting.

www.mjtrim.com
Wide selection of trims and notions including: ribbons, specialty and novelty trims, lace and braided trims, beads, buckles, buttons, cords, fringe, purse handles, rhinestones, tassels, appliqués, chain, books, some craft supplies and accessories, and fashion trend reports accompanied by related product information.

www.ribbonjar.com
A wide variety of ribbons and trims at reasonable prices.

www.rubbermonger.com
Wide variety of stamps.

www.rubbertrouble.com
Offers to create rubber stamps of your original designs at very reasonable prices.

www.sideshowstamps.com
Great selection of retro stamps.

www.tinseltrading.com
Wide variety of high-end notions and trims including many vintage selections and hard-to-find items.

www.wardrobesupplies.com/store
Professional wardrobe-department supplier, featuring sewing notions, tools, dyes, hardware, findings, millinery and jewelry/beading supplies, distressing agents, etc.

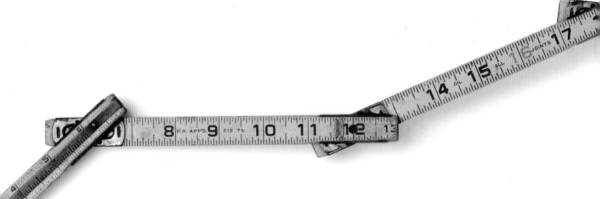